T0332222

Real Business Cases in Strategic Planning

This book shows how systematic strategic planning (SSP) can be used on real-world projects for professionals at any skill level. It illustrates how this systematic methodology and its analysis tools—using workshop and brainstorming approaches—can be easily understood and universally applied to any type of business. Rather than explaining the methodology and its tools, the author succinctly shows how to use the simplified version of his methodology for developing strategic plans. But, perhaps more importantly, the reader is shown how to identify which circumstances require the use of particular tools and also how to target them directly to achieve effective results. The SSP methodology and the use of a workshop approach, real-world strategic planning projects, and working forms are presented to guide the reader through preparing the strategic plan for existing or future business.

The first part of the book provides an overall framework and briefly describes some of the sections of the systematic pattern of strategic planning. In addition, it explains the use of a workshop approach for strategic planning based on SSP principles. The second part details case studies of strategic planning projects from real-world organizations across a variety of industries. Most of the organizations used both the simplified version of the SSP methodology and the techniques, while others benefited strictly from customizing the SSP methodology.

Real Business Cases
in Strategic Planning
A Simplified Methodology for Achieving
Your Organization's Data-Driven Goals

Hakan Butuner

Routledge
Taylor & Francis Group

A PRODUCTIVITY PRESS BOOK

First published 2025
by Routledge
605 Third Avenue, New York, NY 10158

and by Routledge
4 Park Square, Milton Park, Abingdon, Oxon, OX14 4RN

Routledge is an imprint of the Taylor & Francis Group, an informa business

ISBN: 978-1-032-85736-7 (hbk)
ISBN: 978-1-032-85735-0 (pbk)
ISBN: 978-1-003-51961-4 (ebk)

DOI: 10.4324/9781003519614

Typeset in ITC Garamond Std
by KnowledgeWorks Global Ltd.

To my supportive and lovely lifelong partner Muge

Contents

Preface

I felt the need to show how systematic strategic planning (SSP) can be used on real-world projects even by unskilled professionals. Accordingly, I wanted to write this book in order to let this systematic methodology and its analysis tools, using workshop and brainstorming approaches to be easily understood and universally applied to any type of business.

Rather than explaining the methodology and its tools (which has already been done in my previous book called *Systematic Strategic Planning*), I preferred to introduce this book to show how to use the simplified version of this methodology for developing strategic plans. But, perhaps most importantly of all, this book guides you to identify in what circumstances you might use particular tools, shows you how, and helps you target them directly to achieve effective results.

The main headings in this book are listed below. The SSP methodology and the use of the workshop approach, real-world strategic planning projects and working forms presented will guide you through preparing the strategic plan for your existing or future business.

- The first part provides an overall framework and describes briefly some of the sections of the systematic pattern of strategic planning. Additionally, it explains the use of a workshop approach for strategic planning based on SSP principles.
- The second part demonstrates the strategic planning projects issued are related with the real-world organizations that are from a variety of industries. Though for the majority of the organizations, the pattern of the simplified version of SSP methodology and the techniques of it were used, for some only the pattern but not the recommended techniques were applied.

This book is written chiefly for two groups:

■ One is the strategic planner, students and faculty members who are interested in strategic planning. He/she is skilled in planning strategic plans, but may not fully recognize that strategic planning of any business calls together for a different systematic procedure and workshop approach. His conventional approach must be replaced by the broader analysis of a systematic method, his individual and factual analysis of specifics must give way to group opinions and evaluation of convenience or preference.

■ The second group involves the professional – the person not skilled in applying the techniques and systematic procedure of strategic planning together with the use of brainstorming and workshop approach. This second group includes such people as the owner-manager of a small business, the manager who is generally familiar with strategic planning, and the department head who is faced with a job that he plans to do himself.

The content in this book is composed as a result of the conclusions obtained from different real-world application environments of the issue in the subject and by the composition of the cause-and-effect relations of these. In reality, this book is supporting material for my previous books called *Systematic Strategic Planning: A Comprehensive Framework for Implementation, Control, and Evaluation,* and *Case Studies in Strategic Planning.* It has been designed to be specific, simple to understand, and easy to use.

I owe all the participants—including senior managers and related staff from the institutions as well as from their related parties (such as investors, suppliers, customer representatives, etc.), who had contributed within parallel group work sessions through their excellent efforts on the development of the herein-issued strategic planning projects—a great debt of gratitude.

Most of all, for coming up with the hereby systematic methodology for strategic planning, I am very thankful to Richard Muther and his incredible innovation for planners which is called Planning by Design.

Dr. Hakan Butuner

About the Author

Dr. Hakan Butuner has received his B.Sc. in industrial engineering from Middle East Technical University; MBA from Bilkent University; and Ph.D. in engineering management from the University of Missouri-Rolla.

He has been active both in professional and academic responsibilities for several years. Additionally, as an entrepreneur, he has acted as the affiliate of several US consulting companies' industrial management and engineering consulting and training field; and has also built various international franchising businesses. During the same periods, he has lectured in the business schools and/or industrial engineering departments of renowned universities worldwide.

Currently, he is acting as an associate professor at TED University, in addition to running IMECO (Industrial Management and Engineering Consulting, an affiliate of well-known US consulting companies). Additionally, he is the founder-president of the Institute of Industrial & Systems Engineers – Turkish professional chapter; and the board member of the Institute of High-Performance Planners.

During his long career path as an industrial engineering and management professional, consultant, academician, and trainer, he has completed and participated in over 100 professional industrial engineering and management projects (especially in Strategic Planning, Facilities Design, Operations Improvement, and Process Reengineering) and developed and deployed many training programs and workshops to over 200 corporations and universities with several million dollars' worth of result-based solutions.

Also, as a Planning-by-Design-based developer of Systematic Strategic Planning (SSP), Systematic Planning of Business Functions (SPBF) and

Target-Based Systematic Improvement Planning (SIP) methodologies, he has several cited books and papers (especially in Planning by Design, Operations Management and Improvement, Supply Chain Management, and Strategic & Business Planning areas) published by globally recognized publication houses (such as Taylor & Francis, SAGE) and journals.

STRATEGIC PLANNING I

A strategic plan outlines the path between the current status of business and the desired status to achieve. It helps the business to establish its objectives, goals and the decisions to achieve these objectives and goals. It involves a long-term and prospective perspective.

The strategic plan provides guidance for the preparation of functional plans and business budgets in such a manner that they reflect objectives, main goals and main strategies of the strategic plan during the implementation phase, as well as for basing resource allocation on priorities.

Functional plans help in the implementation of strategic plans by organizing and activating specific subunits of the business (marketing, finance, production, etc.) to pursue the business strategy in daily activities. The greatest responsibilities are in the implementation or execution of a strategic plan. Functional plans are more specific than a business strategy to guide functional actions taken in key parts of the company to implement business strategy. Figure I.1 shows the relationship between functional and strategic plans.

In this part, in addition to the brief description of some of the sections of the systematic pattern of strategic planning (SSP), using a workshop approach for strategic planning based on SSP principles is explained.

DOI: 10.4324/9781003519614-1

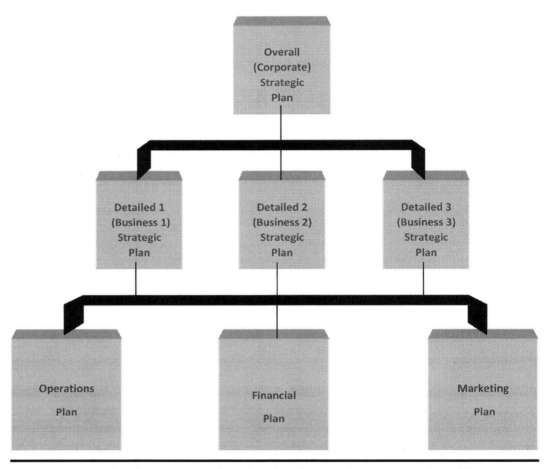

Figure I.1   Relationship between functional and strategic plans (Reprinted from Harrison and St. John, *Foundations in Strategic Management*, Evansville: South-Western Publications, 2001).

Chapter 1

Strategic Planning by Workshop Approach

Workshops are geared toward developing the organization's strategic plans for the next five years. The objective is to:

- Identify the developments and trends in macroeconomic factors that affect the industry most.
- Understand the most influential forces in the industry (customers, suppliers, competitors, related public agencies and organizations, lenders, etc.) and project the positive and negative scenarios to be created by these forces.
- Ascertain the institution's competitive advantages, success factors and key weaknesses.
- Identify the potential opportunities, strategic objectives, primary goals and related key strategies of the institution.

The workshop will also seek to:

- Find out creative, different and better answers to the question of how the prospects for the industry should be and what the role of the institution should be in these prospects.
- Clearly declare relevant goals to the potential organization and members of the institution through a consensus to emerge as a result of brainstorming.

DOI: 10.4324/9781003519614-2

■ Ensure discussion of ideas regarding the subject matter, through a model exercise supportive of developing a democratic platform within the institution.

The moderator manages the work according to the schedule specified below.

Program Contents

1. *Day – Developments (in the World and in Nation)*
   - Strategy development at a glance.
   - Overview of the program's working principles, goals and timetable.
   - Review of trends in macroeconomic, political and other external factors affecting the industry (World, Nation) and effective forces in the industry.
2. *Day – Scenarios, and Evolution and Current State of the Institution*
   - Workshop for identification of positive scenarios for the sector.
   - Presentation and review of positive scenarios.
   - Workshop for identification of negative scenarios for the sector.
   - Presentation and review of negative scenarios.
   - Review of the evolution of the institution and factors to affect its success.
3. *Day – Current State of the Institution*
   - Workshop for identification of the strengths of the institution.
   - Presentation and review of strengths.
   - Workshop for identification of the weaknesses of the institution.
   - Presentation and review of weaknesses.
   - Workshop for identification of competitive advantages and success factors for the institution.
   - Presentation and review of competitive advantages and success factors.
4. *Day – Future Design of the Institution*
   - Workshop for identification of opportunities for the institution.
   - Presentation and review of opportunities.
   - Workshop for identification of strategic objectives and key goals for the institution.
   - Presentation and review of strategic objectives and key goals.
5. *Day – Future Design of the Institution*
   - Workshop for identification of main strategies for the institution.
   - Summary review of works.
   - Organization of study documents.

Participant Profile

The participant profile involving groups with equivalent levels of knowledge and experience but varying perspectives would undoubtedly be very useful in facilitating that all participants express their views and reach a consensus. It is recommended that participants include senior managers and related staff from the institution as well as experienced people from the institution and related parties (stakeholders, suppliers, customer representatives, sector representatives, associations, related public agencies and organizations, etc.). The number of participants in parallel group work sessions should be limited, to ensure efficiency. The proposed number of participants is either 12 or 20.

Methodology and Approach

"Brainstorming" and "Workshop" approaches are used in addition to the SSP methodology throughout this work.

Brainstorming, in its broadest definition, is a participatory and practical approach organized to generate creative ideas. Ideas are generated to reach a solution, support the decision-making process, create a scenario, etc.

It is important to question the assumptions and beliefs that everyone in the organization accepts and discuss what new opportunities can be created if these beliefs change. Since creative thinking is widely dispersed within every organization, it should not only be monopolized by top management, but new and interesting perspectives that have been suppressed and isolated should emerge.

For example, looking at the world from a new perspective, through a new lens, to think about things in the simplest way possible, to redefine and examine them accordingly, in order to create a strategy, makes it easier for us to see the points we cannot see. To this end, brainstorming is an approach that is most appropriate and efficient in such matters.

During the implementation of this approach, participants are expected to wear various hats and make comments on the perspectives given by these hats. These perspectives include being objective, emotional, risk-taking, positive, creatively flighty, and judgmental.

The aim of brainstorming is to create a radical thinking environment, adopt simple and mutual thinking systematics, examine what is accepted and to reach a solution with common sense.

The venue to be selected for the work must be places other than offices, if possible. It must offer an atmosphere to the extent possible. The work must be executed in a disciplined but informal manner.

Following Steps and Required Actions

Following this work, it would be useful to create functional plans to achieve key goals and strategies identified for the future of the company, through a separate activity and/or workshop.

Functional Business Plans should be prepared according to the working content specified below, together with employees deemed appropriate in the relevant units of the organization.

Preparation of functional business plans should be about three to four months, although the project duration varies according to the intensity of project resources, the performance of project workers and the timing of approval processes.

Marketing Plan:

- Market Analysis
- Competitors, Competitive Conditions and Situation Analysis
- Target Markets
- Sales Targets, Strategies and Actions to be Taken

Operations Plan:

- Market Analysis
- Current Technical Capability Analysis
- Envisaged Main Objectives
- Analysis and Feasibility of Required Investments
- Major Required Activities (Organization, Promotion, etc.)
- Anticipated Personnel Needs and Organization

Financial Plan:

- Sales Analysis
- Personnel Analysis
- Operations Analysis
- Investments

- Profit/Loss Statement
- Profit/Loss Analysis
- Balance sheet
- Fund Flow Table
- Opportunity Costs Analysis
- Business Risks
- Financial Analysis

Chapter 2

Systematic Pattern of Strategic Planning

Systematic Strategic Planning (SSP) is the pattern of procedures by which an organization defines its current status, competitive advantages, opportunities, long-term goals and the strategies. SSP is based on the principles of *PxD (Planning by Design)* which is generated by Muther (2011).

SSP (Butuner 2015) consists of a framework of phases through which each project passes, a pattern of sections for straightforward planning, and the fundamentals involved in any strategic planning project. Figure 2.1 illustrates the SSP full version.

The techniques to be used for strategic planning should not be perceived as a procedure of systematic, and the techniques used should be continuously repeatable and modifiable depending on the characteristics of individual cases.

Certain working forms (in the forms of key documents and output) are used in applying the techniques in each section or step of the SSP pattern.

In Phases II and III, the planning specialist follows a method of procedures to achieve alternative strategic plans.

In holdings/large businesses, the planning specialist uses Phase II in the full SSP version to develop an overall strategic plan. Planning specialist may repeat Phase III of the full version to develop detailed strategic plans of each business/division of the holding/large business or may use shortened SSP version instead if the business is small.

Phases II and III pass through the following five sections. Figure 2.2 illustrates the five sections of SSP.

 DOI: 10.4324/9781003519614-3

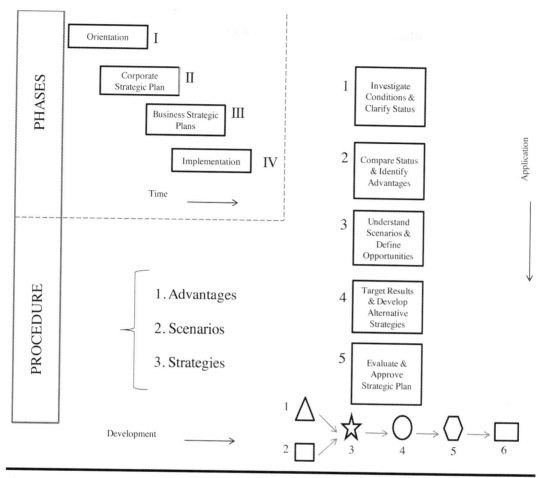

Figure 2.1   SSP – reference table (Butuner 2015).

Investigating Environmental and Internal Conditions

The first section of the SSP is to answer the question *"where are we?"* This requires a comprehensive status analysis. Status analysis essentially covers the following assessments:

- Analysis of the internal structure of the organization (analysis of the duties and authorities, performances, problems, potentials, institutional culture, human resources, technology level, etc. of the organization.)
- Environmental analysis (analysis of external conditions as well as the environment in which the organization operates and related

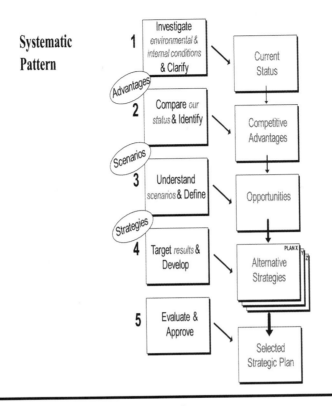

Figure 2.2   SSP – five sections (Butuner 2015).

parties – target group of the organization and parties affected
negatively/positively from the organization's activities.)
◼ Analysis of developments that the organization may face and be
affected in the future.

During and after status analysis, the internal strengths and weaknesses of
the business, and the positive and negative developments originating from
external factors are identified.

Environmental Analysis

Intention of environmental analysis is as follows:

◼ To determine the developments and trends in the macroeconomical
(demographical, economical, judicial-political, technological, socio-
cultural) environment that affects the business and its industry at most.

■ To understand the powers that affect competition in the industry (new businesses, customers, suppliers, substitutes, competitors, government, financial institutions, etc.).

■ To anticipate the trends that these powers would create for the industry.

Environmental analysis, which is illustrated in Figure 2.3, considers the general trends in the world, changes in the environment in which the business operates and particularly the expectations of the group served by the industry. Environmental analysis identifies not only current status but also lays the basis for future forecasts or the creation of scenarios. As long as a business that is in interaction but cannot control many processes in the environment fails to follow up this change, then strategic planning would not make much sense. Key considerations in environmental analysis are as follows:

■ Current global status and development trends in the field of the business.

■ Current domestic status and development trends in the field of the business.

■ Critical issues that closely concern the business among the basic trends and problems in the world and in the country. How and in

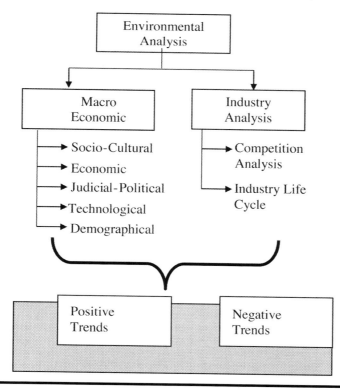

Figure 2.3   Environmental analysis.

what direction these issues will affect the industry in which the business operates.
■ Basic negativities and uncertainties faced by the business due to the conditions of the industry.

Macroeconomic Analysis

Macroeconomic variables are the variables that affect the businesses and their industry, which are not under the control of businesses. Macroeconomic variables are as follows:

■ Demographical
■ Economical
■ Judicial-political
■ Technological
■ Socio-cultural

The variables to be evaluated in order to compose changes and developments are specified below. This review should primarily be conducted at the global scale, and then at regional and country scales.

After collecting information about the present state, efforts must be made to identify trends in variables and the future continuation of these trends. The purpose is to ascertain the impacts of variables in the macroeconomic environment on stakeholders.

In order to analyze the effects of trends and developments within these variables on the industry, "Working forms: Macroeconomic analysis table" can be used. While composing this matrix;

■ on vertical axis – trends determined on variables,
■ on horizontal axis – stakeholders of business,
■ on elements of matrix – the anticipated effects of trends on the stakeholders should be input.

Macroeconomic analysis table summarizes the status of the variables with respect to customers, government, financial institutions, suppliers, shareholders and employees' points of view. If macroeconomic factors will;

■ turn into a better condition than now, then mark as **+,**
■ remain unchanged, then mark as blank,
■ turn into a worse condition than now, and then mark as **−.**

Competition Analysis

Porter (1998) stated that, if a business is producing a product or service with a market, considerations like global and domestic market conditions, development/evolution trends of the demand for the subject product and/or service, price movements, changes in quality and standards, competition, etc. are laid down as a result of a comprehensive analysis of the powers in the industry.

The powers that affect a business at most are the groups that compose competition within the industry:

- Rivalry among existing companies
- Threat of potential new entrants
- Bargaining power of customers
- Threat of substitutes
- Bargaining power of suppliers
- Bargaining power of other stakeholders (government, trade unions, financial institutions, etc.)

The effects of these powers determine the strength of competition within the industry. In an industry where the power of these groups is high, the potential for profitability will be low. When one of these groups has a higher power, this would have negative implications for the industry, whereas a lower power would have positive implications. Now, let's analyze these powers (see Working forms: Competition analysis table):

Rivalry: **Competition in an industry is high if;**

- the number of active businesses is high,
- the growth rate of the industry decelerates or accelerates rapidly,
- the characteristics of products/services are not very different,
- the fixed costs are high,
- cost of leaving industry is high.

Threat of potential new entrants: **Entry barriers are high at the rate;**

- of having low costs due to the size of the companies within the industry,
- of having brands within the industry,
- of having high investment requirements,
- of accessibility to distribution channels being hard,

- of having a high learning curve effect,
- of having various limitations by the government for the new entrants.

Bargaining power of customers: **Customer is powerful if;**

- it purchases in large quantities of the products/services of the supplier,
- it has the potential to produce products/services through vertical integration,
- there are alternative suppliers,
- the cost of changing suppliers is not high,
- it is sensitive to price and service variations,
- the purchased product/service does not bear an importance for its production/operation.

Threat of substitutes: Substitutes are products/services that cover the same requirements in different ways. In industries where substitutes are plenty and the customers have low product changing costs, companies can face less profit.

Bargaining power of suppliers: **Suppliers are powerful if;**

- the industry is composed of limited suppliers,
- their products/services are unique and exclusive,
- there are no substitutes in the market,
- they have the potential to compete with the current customers through vertical integration,
- the purchases compose a small portion of their income.

The results of analyses conducted in the light of these and similar considerations will be given in summary (Porter 1998):

- Each force needs to be evaluated in terms of – does it make the market;
  - high,
  - moderate or,
  - low attractiveness?
- Each force needs to be evaluated in terms of its relative importance.

When the industry changes significantly it is frequently not because of one competitive force, but because of changes to two or possibly three forces combining together.

Industry Life Cycle

Vernon (1979) stated that each industry passes through the phases of introduction, growth, maturity and finally regression. The phase that the industry is within facilitates the estimation of impacts and trends of powers defined in competition analysis. Figure 2.4 shows the industry life cycle.

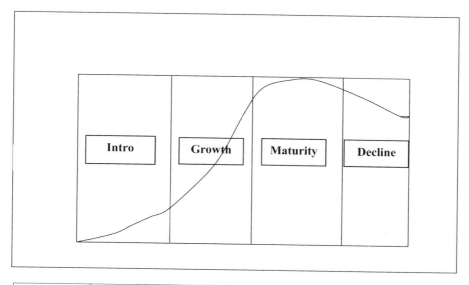

	Intro	Growth	Maturity	Decline
Sales	Low	Rapidly Growing	Peak	Declining
Cost	High/ Customer	Moderate/ Customer	Low/Customer	Low/Customer
Profit	Loss	Growing	High	Declining
Competition	Low	Growing	Fixed or Declining	Declining

Figure 2.4 Industry life cycle (Reprinted from Raymond Vernon, "The product cycle hypothesis in a new international environment," *Oxford Bulletin of Economics and Statistics* **41, no. 4 (1979): 255–267).**

Internal Analysis

While an internal status analysis is performed within the business, the past performance of the business is evaluated, and its strengths and weaknesses are put forth. The purpose is to identify the potential of the business taking into consideration its existing performance and problems.

Diagnosing a business' key strengths and weaknesses requires the adoption of a disaggregated view of the business. Examining the business across distinct functional areas is one way to disaggregate the business for internal analysis purposes (see Working forms: Functional approach table).

Therefore, the business should examine past performance (see Working forms: Business history summary table) to isolate key internal contributors to favorable (or unfavorable) results. What did we do well, or poorly, in marketing operations, financial operations, and financial management that had a major influence on past results? Was the sales force effectively organized? Were we in the right channels of distribution? Did we have the financial resources to support the past strategy? The same examination and questions can be applied to the business's current situation, with particular emphasis on changes in the importance of key dimensions over time.

Quantitative tools cannot be applied to all internal factors, and the judgments of key planning participants may be used in the evaluation. Company or product image and prestige are examples of internal factors more appropriate for qualitative evaluation.

The considerations revealed by the Functional Approach are grouped under various functional headings such as overall management, human resources, operations/technology, marketing, finance and accounting, and their distinction as things done well and poorly.

Identification of Competitive Advantages

The organization's strengths and weaknesses are compared with the key factors in the market development phases, capacities and resources of main competitors and the industry's success factors, to identify competitive advantages. Figure 2.5 summarizes the development of a business profile (Pearce and Robinson 2011).

The result of the second step should be a determination of whether key internal factors are (see Working forms: Comparison with main competitors

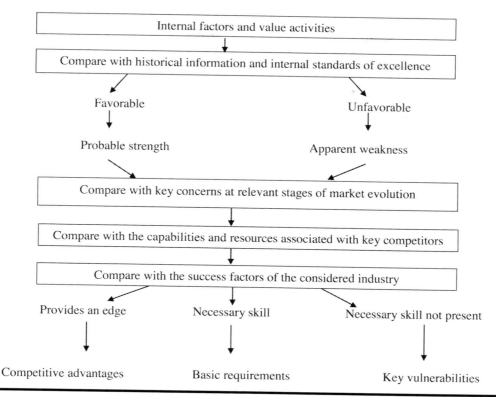

Figure 2.5 Competitive advantages and success factors (Reprinted from Pearce and Robinson, *Strategic management: Formulation, implementation and control* (Columbus: McGraw-Hill Higher Education, 2011)).

and industry average, and competitive advantages – success factors – key weaknesses tables):

a. Competitive advantages – factors providing the business with an edge compared to its competitors, and therefore key factors around which to build the business strategy.

b. Success factors – factors that are important capabilities for the business to have but are also typical of every viable competitor. Does not represent a potential source of any strategic advantage.

c. Key vulnerabilities – factors on which the business currently lacks the necessary skill, knowledge, or resources to compete effectively. This assessment is also a key input because businesses will want to avoid choosing strategies that depend on factors in this category. Businesses usually target key vulnerabilities as areas for special attention to remediate and change this situation.

Understand Scenarios and Define Opportunities

Figure 2.6 shows the procedure for identifying opportunities.

Scenarios

First of all, the scenarios to be created by trends revealed by environmental analysis for the industry must be developed; i.e. alternative scenarios must be developed for the future. Thus, assumptions are grouped under various scenarios, their potential positive and negative impacts on the industry are

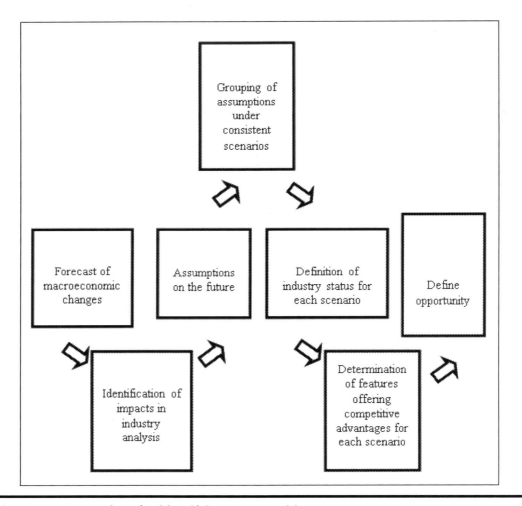

Figure 2.6 Procedure for identifying opportunities (Butuner 2015).

identified, and the potential status in the industry is defined. The scenarios are as follows:

- Internally consistent views of the future.
- Focus on discontinuity and change.
- Explore the impact of the change on key players and how they respond to the environment.

The opportunities and threats that may be offered and posed for the organization by positive and negative scenarios revealed by scenario analysis must be identified. Furthermore, the identification of the organization's competitive advantages and weaknesses relative to competitors and industry standards could lead this section to an efficient result.

In short, in order to identify opportunities and threats, the organization's competitive advantages and weaknesses must be matched with potential positive (attractive) and negative (risky) scenarios that may be encountered in the industry.

Assumptions imply the external factors that are not under the direct control of the business preparing the strategic plan but that can affect the progress and success of the strategic plan. After reviewing socio-cultural factors, technological factors, political environmental, legal conditions, macroeconomic factors and variables originating from the international system in the environmental analysis, the tendencies of related parties such as competitors, customers and suppliers must reflect onto the systematic strategic planning as assumptions.

First, key external variables are identified. Assumptions are made for the values of quantitative and qualitative variables (through brainstorming or statistical models.) Brainstorming and/or statistical models are popular estimation techniques:

- Brainstorming is a non-numerical estimation technique. While conducting scenario analysis, instruments like participatory meetings bringing together various groups concerning the business are used. For the efforts to be made in this scope, it is possible to outsource specialized services, such as the use of facilitators (moderators) who will neutrally facilitate participatory meetings.
- Statistical models are numerical techniques including relations and other econometric models. However, it is based on historical data, and the error margin increases as the structure of relations changes in time.

Grouping of assumptions by positioning the key assumptions which underlies the basics of an issue. Generate scenario stories by testing out judgments and identifying interdependencies.

Opportunities and Threats

The opportunities and threats that may be offered and posed for the business under the positive and negative scenarios to come out from scenario analysis must be identified. Moreover, determining the strengths and weaknesses of the company compared to its competitors will be able to carry the analysis to a satisfactory result. In short, competitive advantages and weaknesses of the business need to be matched with the potential positive (attractive) and negative (risky) scenarios in the industry (see Working forms: Opportunities – Matching Competitive Advantages with Positive Scenarios).

While developing strategies for the future, opportunities will have a significant influence while threats will be monitored closely by the business and measures will be taken against these threats.

Opportunities, by definition, arise in cases where the unresolved problems and unsatisfied expectations and needs are identified for the use of products and/or services in the market, and if solutions can be produced for these.

By testing out total market attractiveness of each positive scenario, you would be able to screen out investment opportunities even before considering what kind of competitive strengths you might be able to attain. The *attractiveness* is the net benefits less the costs (not just the benefits.)

Besides market attractiveness of a scenario, to position a business effectively you also need to take some view of its competitive position with respect to the particular scenario.

Not all opportunities are equally valuable. A business with limited resources cannot pursue every opportunity with which it is faced. It must select those opportunities which are going to be the most rewarding. The key decisions in screening and selecting opportunities relate to the size of the opportunity, the investment necessary to exploit it, the rewards that will be gained and the risks likely to be encountered.

Strategic Objectives, Main Goals, and Main Strategies

Strategic Objectives

Strategic objectives are the conceptual results that the business aims to achieve within a certain timeframe. Strategic objectives and main goals answer the question *"what do we want to achieve?"* within the strategic systematic planning.

Main Goals

Main goals are specific and measurable sub-objectives specified for the achievement of strategic objectives. Unlike strategic objectives, goals are expressed in quantifiable terms and cover a shorter term. Multiple goals may be established to achieve a strategic objective.

Main goals are the qualitative and quantitative expression of strategic objectives within a defined timeframe (see Working forms: Strategic objectives and goals). For this reason, they are measurable sub-objectives intended for outputs to be achieved. Goals should be expressed in terms of quantity, cost, quality and time.

Main Strategies

Strategies are instruments for the achievement of long-term goals. It is a course of action selected from a series of options in order to achieve a goal established against uncertainties.

Alternative strategies are developed by searching for an answer to the question *"what should businesses do to be competitive and lasting in their own industries and markets?"*

Determination of a suitable strategy for a business begins with identifying the opportunities and risks in its environment. This (discussion) is concerned with the identification of a range of alternative strategies, the narrowing of this range by recognizing the constraints imposed by business capability, and the determination of one or more strategies at acceptable levels of risk. While evaluating the opportunities defined on the basis of analyses conducted, various strategies we can implement come out:

■ You should have a single strategy for a single opportunity.
■ If there are multiple opportunities, you can have multiple strategies.

Based on using both the techniques of Generic Competitive Strategies and Components of Strategy, the main strategy(ies) can be identified. Accordingly, this will lead you to the selection of the corresponding Grand Strategy(ies.)

Generic Competitive Strategies

The fundamental basis of above-average performance in the long run is *sustainable competitive advantage*. There are two basic types of competitive advantage a business can possess: low cost or differentiation. Any strengths or weaknesses is ultimately a function of relative cost or differentiation (Porter 1998).

The two basic types of competitive advantage combined with the scope of activities for which a business seeks to achieve them lead to three *generic strategies* for achieving above-average performance in an industry (see Working forms: Generic competitive strategies).

Each involves a different route to competitive advantage, combining the competitive advantage sought with the scope of the target. The specific actions required for each generic strategy vary widely from industry to industry. Broad target is defined as one which;

1. covers a great diversity of customer needs and market segments, or
2. covers a wide and perhaps complex range of products and services, or
3. covers both (1) and (2).

Components of Strategy

In conjunction with its objectives the firm may choose one, two, or all of the strategy components with respect to its current product-market position (Ansoff 1970). This can be illustrated by means of a matrix (see Working forms: Components of strategy).

Grand Strategies

Grand strategies often called business strategies provide basic direction for strategic actions. Grand strategies indicate how long-range objectives will be achieved. Thus, a grand strategy can be defined as a comprehensive general approach that guides major actions:

■ Are we going to stay in the same ring of value chain? Are we going to continue doing the same work with the same system? (Constancy)
■ Are we going to enter new business areas with additional functions, products and/or markets? (Expansion)
■ Are we going to leave the business completely? Are we going to leave some of the business? (Reduction)

Any one of the 12 principal grand strategies (Pearce and Robinson 2011) serves as the basis for achieving major long-term objectives of a business, identified according to the techniques of Generic Competitive Strategies and Components of Strategies:

- Concentration
- Market Development
- Product Development
- Innovation
- Horizontal Integration
- Vertical Integration
- Joint Venture
- Concentric Diversification
- Conglomerate Diversification
- Retrenchment/Turnaround
- Divestiture
- Liquidation

Chapter 3

Brainstorming

Brainstorming (BS), with the extensive definition, is a form of meeting arranged to produce creative ideas. The ideas produced are intended to reach a solution, support the decision-making process, compose scenarios, and/or find out competitive advantages, etc. BS is actually a participative and practical technique commonly used in order to let the organizations develop strategies to reach an efficient and profitable structure.

The intention of BS is to create a radical thinking environment, adopt a simple and mutual systematic thinking, examine agreements and assumptions and reach a solution by consensus.

 DOI: 10.4324/9781003519614-4

Preparatory Work

- In order to manage BS, it will be beneficial to;
  - reach a required solution by BS, in other words, to reveal the intention of BS,
  - determine the sources of the results required to be reached,
  - well understand and define the problems to be solved,
  - determine the developments and trends on the issues to be addressed.
- The trends, opinions and ideas to be evaluated can cover the following aspects of the issue;
  - history,
  - current condition,
  - future,
  - significant and global trends,
  - main trends and generally agreed concepts,
  - issues beyond normal that raise interest.
- It is beneficial to perform a status analysis regarding the issue before starting BS.

Pre-Meeting

If possible, locations besides offices shall be selected for the meeting. The location selected for BS shall be indoor and isolated as much as possible.

It will be beneficial to inform the individuals, who will participate in the meeting, beforehand regarding the issue and to give a specific period – such as one week – to have them think, practice and generate ideas on the issue.

As this approach will enable the participants to generate more ideas during BS, it may also lead to participants influencing each other through pre-meeting discussions., so informing the participants beforehand shall be left to the decision of the meeting manager.

BS Meeting

BS meetings shall be held in a disciplined environment but away from formality. The number of individuals attending the BS meetings shall not be excessive and it shall be limited according to the intention of BS, meeting hall, and time to be allocated for the meeting. The participants of equal levels of knowledge and experience will be beneficial for everyone to make their point.

BS meetings shall be active, alive and loud as much as possible. It will be beneficial to have the BS meetings managed by a meeting manager.

While starting the BS meeting, even if the attendants experienced in the subject area is not necessary it is recommended. This condition will provide benefits for the success of BS and for reaching the right solution.

Recorder shall not be used during the BS, as the participants would not like it. Everyone should actively participate in the sessions.

Start of Meeting

Before starting BS, the meeting manager shall clearly communicate to the participants about the intention of the meeting, the result required to be obtained, and the source of the result required to be obtained.

The meeting manager shall enlighten the participants regarding the sections of the meeting and the length of each section. This will make the meeting more efficient. Being adhered to time is the duty of the meeting manager.

For a positive start of BS, the meeting manager should start with the entertaining and interesting questions. At the beginning, written expression of the opinions is recommended in respect of accelerating the adaptation process of the participants.

Generating Ideas

Speaking rights should be given to the participants in a disorderly manner. Here, the important thing is to provide everyone to tell their opinions (the approach that is mostly recommended).

It is required that everyone shall speak in turns and present all kinds of their opinions regarding the issue without being interrupted. A specific idea is selected and other ideas evoking the idea are encouraged.

Thinking positively and then negatively by expressing their ideas in these directions is required from the participants (*parallel thinking*).

As an extension of the *parallel thinking* approach, the six-hat method of *Edward de Bono* can be used. During the application of this method, it is expected that the participants wear various hats and make interpretations over the perspectives given by these hats. These perspectives are as follows; being objective, being emotional, being a risk taker, being positive, being a creative freak and being judgmental.

During BS, the meeting manager shall provide an environment for all the participants to speak. Here, the point not to be ignored is that the silence of the participants arises from their thinking requirements, being unable to leave their shyness at first, from their mistrust against the environment, etc. The meeting manager shall specify the ideas by repetition. Differences can arise on the second expression of an idea.

During the generation of ideas, the meeting manager shall not make any interpretations, criticisms or be involved in evaluations. The meeting manager shall accept the ideas with maturity. Even superficial-seeming ideas can contribute to the emergence of concepts that will lead to a real result.

Providing not to diverge from the issue during the generation of ideas or assembling the diverged issue is the duty of the meeting manager. Meeting manager can ask questions such as *how, where, when, why* in order to accelerate the meeting.

Meeting manager shall remind the intention of the meeting during BS. When the definition of intention by the first BS is not able to assist on generation of ideas, a second definition shall be selected.

A work session that turned to be inefficient shall not be pushed to continue. It is beneficial to conclude the BS sessions with the most unimagined ideas. This will assist the rise of different ideas.

During BS all ideas shall be numbered and written on a *flip chart* by the meeting manager. The writing shall be with a pen that is non-erasable and that attracts everyone's attention. All ideas shall be placed on the wall side to side to allow everyone to see. During writing, it is important not to spoil the fluency of BS and to use abbreviations in order to provide the rise of new ideas.

Evaluation of Ideas

Elimination is applied on all the assembled ideas. In order to facilitate the elimination, the assembled list should be allocated to subgroups (economic, social, technological, legal, etc.). It will be beneficial to perform the elimination of the participants.

During the elimination, the meeting manager can use various techniques. For example, the ideas being really critical and being impossible to be estimated and that can't be controlled can be kept and the others can be removed from the list according to the requirements of the meeting manager.

Developing Scenarios

Participants shall be grouped by the meeting manager in different rooms in order to develop scenario drafts. Each group can have the eliminated list of the scenarios.

Scenarios are developed by the groups on the progress of the addressed issue by following the list if a list is given, or by requiring the groups to keep the ideas in their memory if a list is not given.

The scenarios developed shall be consolidated by the relevant teams during the breaks and a common direction shall be obtained from the scenarios. At the last point, a common scenario should be formed.

Chapter 4

Preparation for Workshops

Before starting the workshop, it is useful to determine the developments in the macroeconomic forces that affect the sector the most and their impact on the sector, to understand the effective forces in the industry (customers, suppliers, competitors, etc.) and to analyze the situation related to the organization. Before the workshop, it is helpful to inform the participants of the questions in advance and give them a certain amount of time – such as a week – to think and work on them. Since this situation may enable the participants to generate more ideas during the workshop and may also cause the participants to influence each other by discussing among themselves before the workshop, it should be left to the moderator's decision to give advance notice.

Macroeconomic Analysis

Variables that need to be examined in order to determine the developments in macroeconomic forces (world, country) and their effects on the sector (see Working forms: Macroeconomic analysis worksheet at Butuner 2015):

- Demographic variables
- Legal-political variables
- Economic variables
- Socio-cultural variables
- Technological variables

DOI: 10.4324/9781003519614-5

Industry Forces

Questions to be answered in order to understand the influential forces in the industry (customers, suppliers, competitors, etc.) (Wickham 2004:)

Industry Information

Industry is defined as a group of enterprises that produce similar products or services.

- How is the industry defined?
- The size of the industry.
- Significant industry diffractions.
- Overall growth rate.
- How much should be devoted to creationism?
- Significant improvements in consumer behavior and shopping habits.
- Technological advances in product, service, distribution and operations.
- How long can the opportunity be seized?
- How long will customers stay engaged?
- What is the value-added chain in the industry?
- What are the inputs and outputs of each link of the value-added chain?
- What are the trends and developments that shape the industry in the world?
- What are the trends driving the industry in the country?
- What are the critical success indicators in the industry?
- Where is the industry headed?
- How is the industry changing with technology?

Competitors, Competitive Conditions

- The basis of competition in the industry.
- Price, product diversification, differentiation and the importance of branding.
- Who are the leaders in the industry?
- Who are the most high-tech businesses?
- Who are the businesses that produce/serve the cheapest?
- What customer segments do key businesses affect?
- What are the features of preferring businesses? Compare (price, service…)
- Those who receive customer loyalty from businesses?

- Growth rates of important enterprises, market shares.
- What are the resources (facilities, buildings, capital) used by important businesses?
- How many businesses account for 80% of industry turnover?
- Is there a cartel in the industry?
- Capacity, turnover and growth rate of supply in the industry?
- Is the product imported? What is the import price and quality?
- Market shares of products?
- Considering the product life cycle, what stage do you put the products in?
- How is the differentiation of products in the industry? Is this differentiation reflected in the product price?
- Fixed and variable expense ratios of enterprises in industry?
- What is the percentage of capacity utilization in the industry?
- The effect of capacity utilization rate on prices?
- Exit costs from the industry?
- Are there any businesses coming out of the industry?
- Have there been any business marriages in the industry recently?
- What are the new entrants to the industry?
- What are the turnover and growth rates of new entrants to the industry?
- What is the investment capital required to enter the industry?
- Are there multinational businesses planning or entering the industry?
- The "Learning Curve" effect?
- Making it difficult for the new entrant to the industry to enter; Are there any factors such as patented products, mastery of distribution channels, certificate of competence?
- Government restrictions on entry into industry?

Customers

- How is the industry distributed across different sectors?
- Who are the customers? Who is not a customer?
- In how many segments are customers collected?
- What are the top five expectations of customers in order of importance? To what extent can these expectations be met?
- In which areas do customers operate?
- What makes customers important and exclusive?
- What are the causes of customer complaints?
- What is the geographical distribution of customers?
- How is the income/education/age/status of customers?

- Who is most influenced by the customer when making a purchase decision?
- How do demands vary?
- The cost of the customer's vendor replacement?
- Are there any of the customers who are involved or have any inclinations to manufacture in the industry?
- Through which distribution channels are customers reached? Their accessibility?

The Threat of Substitute Products

- Are there alternatives in the industry to replace the products?
- What is the development trend of alternative products in the industry?
- Who are the customers of these alternative products?
- Product replacement costs for customers?
- What are the effects of substitute products on the product's main prices?

Suppliers

- Who are the suppliers? Who is not a supplier?
- The number of suppliers in the industry and their place of production.
- Suppliers' market shares.
- Do they have their own unique products?
- Do they have the potential to produce products through integration?
- Raw material sources, characteristics and expenses?
- Has a supplier taken business from the industry?
- Are there partnerships or coalitions between suppliers and businesses in the industry?
- What percentage of the production cost do products purchased from suppliers make?
- What is the importance of businesses in the industry for the supplier?
- To what extent are suppliers able to meet expectations?
- What are the most important complaints about suppliers?
- Is changing suppliers a challenge?
- How is the communication with the suppliers?
- What is the ratio of domestic market purchases to imports?
- From which countries are imports made?

Business Risks

- How valid are the estimates about the size of the opportunity?
- How accurate is the data on the industry?
- How were competitors' products evaluated?
- What happens if customers don't find the products as attractive as expected?
- What will happen if opponents become more aggressive than expected?
- Have all competitors been considered?
- How will they respond in principle?
- How can they respond in practice?
- What are the factors that must be provided in order to be successful?
- Are external factors likely to affect profitability?
- Is it possible to take measures to eliminate the identified risks?
- If necessary, can additional resources be transferred?
- Will it be sourced internally or from investors?
- How should investors prepare for the possibility of a shift in expectations?
- Under what circumstances might investors want to exit?

Internal Analysis

In order to analyze the situation related to the organization, the issues that need to be answered are mostly the stages passed from the past to the present and the current performance situations on the basis of the organizational functions they have created in the organization. Things to consider in this regard are the internal factors, such as manpower, technology, organization and management, operational considerations, and products and their position in the market (see Working forms: Functional approach table at Butuner 2015).

Chapter 5

Sample Outline
for Strategic Plan

A good strategic plan is between 25 and 50 pages long and least six months to write.

Executive Summary

This section should summarize the most important subjects of the strategic plan and interconnect various sections. Begin with a two-page or three-page management summary of the venture. Include a short description of the business, and discuss major goals and objectives. Describe company operations to date, potential legal considerations, and areas of risk and opportunity.

Strategic Plan

1. *Status Analysis*
   The status analysis section is expected not to exceed three pages.

   Environmental analysis:
   This should consider external factors such as demographical, economical, legal-political, technological and social changes, market dynamics, customer expectations, competitive conditions, strategies and objectives of competitors, suppliers, substitutes, etc.

                                                    DOI: 10.4324/9781003519614-6

- Macroeconomic analysis (global, national)
  - Demographical variables
  - Judicial-political variables
  - Economic variables
  - Socio-cultural variables
  - Technological variables
- Competition analysis
  - Rivalry
  - Suppliers
  - Customers
  - Substitutes
  - New arrivals
- Industry life cycle

Internal analysis – business strengths and weaknesses:
The phases of evolution experienced by the business from the past till today and the strengths and weaknesses caused by them on your business structure must be mentioned. This should consider such internal factors as labor force, technology, organization and management, operational matters, products and their market positions, financial characteristics, etc.

2. *Competitive Advantages, Success Factors and Weaknesses*
3. *Scenarios and Opportunities*

Positive and negative scenarios for industry:
The potential positive and negative scenarios for your industry for the next five years must be mentioned, taking into consideration the major developments in your respective industry worldwide and in the nation.

Business opportunities and threats

4. *Strategic Objectives, Main Goals, Grand Strategies*
The goals intended to be achieved during the next five years must be mentioned for each year, taking into consideration the following headings:

Strategic objectives
Main goals:
- Financial and marketing goals:
  - Which countries to be in
  - Regional concentration
  - Planned strategic partnerships

- Alliances, merging and acquisitions, etc.
- Market goals
- Financial goals, etc.
  - Operational goals:
    - Technological improvements
    - Organization, etc.

Grand strategies

Appendix

Provide a bibliography of all the reference materials you consulted.

Chapter 6

Working Forms

Following this sheet are copies of the forms used for SSP. They may be used when solving your next strategic planning problem. You may reproduce the copies of these forms for your own use, provided you recognize their original source and hold their use within the copyright restrictions covering this book. Each of the forms included in this section is explained in the text and is listed in its order of appearance in the text.

Form Code	Form Title
IMECO – SSP – BH1	Business History Summary Table
IMECO – SSP – FA1	Internal Analysis-Functional Approach
IMECO – SSP – ME1	Macro-Economic Analysis Form
SSP – CA1	Competition Analysis Form
IMECO – SSP – CC1	Comparison with Competitors & Ind.Avg.
IMECO – SSP – CW1	Competitive Advantages-Success Factors–Key Vulnerabilities
IMECO – SSP – MCS1	Opportunities – Matching Competitive Advantages with Positive Scenarios
IMECO - SSP – OG1	Strategic Objectives–Goals
SSP – CS1	Components of Strategy
SSP – GS1	Generic Competitive Strategies

DOI: 10.4324/9781003519614-7

Business History Summary

Prepared by: _____ .   Business: _____ .

Authorized by: _____ .   Project: _____ Date: _____ .

	Year	Year	Year	Year	Year	Year
PERSONNEL						
TECHNICAL						
ORGANIZATION and GENERAL MANAGEMENT						
PRODUCTION/ OPERATIONS						
MARKETING						
FINACE and ACCOUNTING (x1000)						

IMECO - SSP – BH1

Functional Approach

Prepared by: _____. Business: _____.

Authorized by: _____. Project: _____. Date: _____.

	FACTORS	Strengths/Weaknesses
MARKETING	Firm's products/services; breadth of product line	
	Concentration of sales in a few products or to a few customers	
	Ability to gather needed information about markets	
	Market share or submarket shares	
	Product/service mix and expansion potential	
	Channels of distribution: number, coverage and control	
	Effective sales organization	
	Product/service image, reputation and quality	
	Imaginative, efficient and effective sales promotion and advertising	
	Pricing strategy and pricing flexibility	
	Procedures for digesting market feedback and developing new products, services or markets	
	After-sale service and follow up	
	Goodwill/brand loyalty	
FINANCE AND ACCOUNTING	Ability to raise short-term capital	
	Ability to raise long-term capital: debt/equity	
	Corporate-level resources	
	Cost of capital relative to industry and competitors	
	Tax considerations	
	Relations with owners, investors and stockholders	
	Leverage positions	
	Cost of entry and barriers to entry	
	Price-earnings ratio	
	Working capital; flexibility of capital structure	
	Effective cost control, ability to reduce costs	
	Financial size	
	Efficient and effective accounting system for cost, budget and profit planning	

(Continued)

		FACTORS	Strengths/Weaknesses
PRODUCTION/OPERATIONS/ TECHNICAL		Raw materials cost and availability	
		Inventory control systems; inventory turnover	
		Location of facilities; layout and utilization of facilities	
		Economies of scale	
		Technical efficiency of facilities and utilization of capacity	
		Effective use of subcontracting	
		Degree of vertical integration, value added and profit margin	
		Efficiency and cost/benefit of equipment	
		Effective operation control procedures	
		Cost and technological competencies relative to industry and competitors	
		Research and development/technology/innovation	
		Patents, trademarks and similar legal protection	
PERSONNEL		Management personnel	
		Employees' skill and morale	
		Labor relations compared to industry and competition	
		Efficient and effective personnel policies	
		Effective use of incentives to motivate performance	
		Ability to level peaks and valleys of employment	
		Employee turnover and absenteeism	
		Specialized skills	
		Experience	
ORGANIZATION AND GENERAL MANAGEMENT		Organizational structure	
		Firm's image and prestige	
		Firm's record for achieving objectives	
		Organization of communication system	
		Overall organizational control system	
		Organizational climate, culture	
		Use of systematic procedures and techniques in decision making	
		Top-management skill, capacities and interest	
		Strategic planning system	
		Intraorganizational synergy	

IMECO - SSP – FA1

Macro-Economic Analysis Form

Prepared by: _____   Business: _____

Authorized by: _____   Project: _____   Date: _____

	DEMOGRAPH					ECONOMICAL								JUDICIAL - POLITICAL						TECHNOLOGICAL						SOCIO - CULTURAL			
	Population growth	Age pattern	Immigration trends	Birth and death ratios	Education level	Change in GDP	Income distribution	Interest rates	Supply of cash	Inflation rate	Unemployment rate	Foreign exchange policy	Saving&consuming trends	Tax laws	Antitrust law	Incentives	Green laws	Business law	Political stability	R&D expenditures	Innovation opportunities	New products	Acceleration - tech. change	Fastness product supply	Increase in automation	Changes in life styles	Expectancy for career	Change in family structure	Changes in personal values
CUSTOMERS																													
GOVERNMENT																													
FINANCIAL INSTITUTIONS																													
SUPPLIERS																													
SHARE HOLDERS																													
EMPLOYEES																													
RESULT																													

+	Change for the better
	Same as before
–	Change for the worse

IMECO - SSP - ME1

Competition Analysis Form

Prepared by: _____.   Business: _____.

Authorized by: _____.   Project: _____ Date: _____.

	FIRMS IN THE INDUSTRY					THREATS OF NEW COMPANIES						COMPETITIVE POWER OF CUSTOMERS						COMPETITIVE POWER OF SUPPLIERS			
	Quantity of firms in the industry	Growth rate of the industry	Differences and the specialties of the products	Fixed costs	Cost to leave the industry	Costs of the companies in the industry related with the company size	Firms which have the customer-firm loyalty	The equity needed to enter the industry	Ability to reach channel of distribution	Cost advantage related with experience	Barriers to enter the industry	The share of the customer in the whole sale	Potential of production of the products by integration	Alternative suppliers	Cost of the change of the suppliers	Flexibility in the prices	The importance of the product for the customers	Quantity of firms in the industry and the production place	Unique products sale	Substitute goods in the market	Potential of production of the products by integration	The share of the sale of the supplier
Low																						
Avg.																						
High																						

SSP – CA1

Comparison with Main Competitors and Industry Average

Prepared by: _____. Business: _____.

Authorized by: _____. Project: _____ Date: _____.

	FACTORS	OUR BUSINESS	MAIN COMPETITOR(S)	INDUSTRY
MARKETING	Firm's products/services; breadth of product line			
	Concentration of sales in a few products or to a few customers			
	Ability to gather needed information about markets			
	Market share or submarket shares			
	Product/service mix and expansion potential			
	Channels of distribution: number, coverage and control			
	Effective sales organization			
	Product/service image, reputation and quality			
	Imaginative, efficient and effective sales promotion and advertising			
	Pricing strategy and pricing flexibility			
	Procedures for digesting market feedback and developing new products, services or markets			
	After-sale service and follow up			
	Goodwill/brand loyalty			
FINANCE AND ACCUONTING	Ability to raise short-term capital			
	Ability to raise long-term capital: debt/equity			
	Corporate-level resources			
	Cost of capital relative to industry and competitors			
	Tax considerations			
	Relations with owners, investors and stockholders			
	Leverage positions			
	Cost of entry and barriers to entry			
	Price-earnings ratio			
	Working capital; flexibility of capital structure			
	Effective cost control, ability to reduce costs			
	Financial size			
	Efficient and effective accounting system for cost, budget and profit planning			

(Continued)

	FACTORS	OUR BUSINESS	MAIN COMPETITOR(S)	INDUSTRY
PRODUCTION/TECHNICAL	Raw materials cost and availability			
	Inventory control systems; inventory turnover			
	Location of facilities; layout and utilization			
	Economies of scale			
	Technical efficiency of facilities and utilization of capacity			
	Effective use of subcontracting			
	Degree of vertical integration, value added and profit margin			
	Efficiency and cost/benefit of equipment			
	Effective operation control procedures			
	Cost and technological competencies relative to industry and competitors			
	Research and development/technology/ innovation			
	Patents, trademarks and similar			
PERSONNEL	Management personnel			
	Employees' skill and morale			
	Labor relations compared to industry and competition			
	Efficient and effective personnel policies			
	Effective use of incentives to motivate performance			
	Ability to level peaks and valleys of employment			
	Employee turnover and absenteeism			
	Specialized skills			
	Experience			
ORGANIZATION OF GENERAL MANAGEMENT	Organizational structure			
	Firm's image and prestige			
	Firm's record for achieving objectives			
	Organization of communication system			
	Overall organizational control system			
	Organizational climate, culture			
	Use of systematic procedures and techniques			
	Top-management skill, capacities and interest			
	Strategic planning system			
	Intraorganizational synergy			

IMECO - SSP – CC1

Competitive Advantages – Success Factors – Key Vulnerabilities

Prepared by: _____. Business: _____.

Authorized by: _____. Project: _____ Date: _____.

	FACTORS	COMP. ADVANTAGES	SUCCESS FACTORS	KEY WEAKNESSES
MARKETING	Firm's products/services; breadth of product line			
	Concentration of sales in a few products or to a few customers			
	Ability to gather needed information about markets			
	Market share or submarket shares			
	Product/service mix and expansion potential			
	Channels of distribution: number, coverage and control			
	Effective sales organization			
	Product/service image, reputation and quality			
	Imaginative, efficient and effective sales promotion and advertising			
	Pricing strategy and pricing flexibility			
	Procedures for digesting market feedback and developing new products, services or markets			
	After-sale service and follow up			
	Goodwill/brand loyalty			
FINANCE AND ACCUONTING	Ability to raise short-term capital			
	Ability to raise long-term capital: debt/equity			
	Corporate-level resources			
	Cost of capital relative to industry and competitors			
	Tax considerations			
	Relations with owners, investors and stockholders			
	Leverage positions			
	Cost of entry and barriers to entry			
	Price-earnings ratio			
	Working capital; flexibility of capital structure			
	Effective cost control, ability to reduce costs			
	Financial size			
	Efficient and effective accounting system for cost, budget and profit planning			

(Continued)

	FACTORS	COMP. ADVANTAGES	SUCCESS FACTORS	KEY WEAKNESSES
PRODUCTION/TECHNICAL	Raw materials cost and availability			
	Inventory control systems; inventory turnover			
	Location of facilities; layout and utilization			
	Economies of scale			
	Technical efficiency of facilities and utilization of capacity			
	Effective use of subcontracting			
	Degree of vertical integration, value added and profit margin			
	Efficiency and cost/benefit of equipment			
	Effective operation control procedures			
	Cost and technological competencies relative to industry and competitors			
	Research and development/technology/ innovation			
	Patents, trademarks and similar			
PERSONNEL	Management personnel			
	Employees' skill and morale			
	Labor relations compared to industry and competition			
	Efficient and effective personnel policies			
	Effective use of incentives to motivate performance			
	Ability to level peaks and valleys of employment			
	Employee turnover and absenteeism			
	Specialized skills			
	Experience			
ORGANIZATION OF GENERAL MANAGEMENT	Organizational structure			
	Firm's image and prestige			
	Firm's record for achieving objectives			
	Organization of communication system			
	Overall organizational control system			
	Organizational climate, culture			
	Use of systematic procedures and techniques			
	Top-management skill, capacities and interest			
	Strategic planning system			
	Intraorganizational synergy			

IMECO - SSP – CW1

Opportunities – Matching Competitive Advantages with Positive Scenarios

Prepared by: _____. Business: _____.

Authorized by: _____. Project: _____ Date: _____.

	Positive Scenarios Definition	Code of Competitive Advantages	Definition of Opportunities	Reactions of Competitors
Scenario A				
Scenario B				
Scenario C				
Scenario D				

IMECO - SSP – MCS1

Strategic Objectives – Goals

Prepared by: _____.   Business: _____.

Authorized by: _____.   Project: _____ Date: _____.

Opportunity

Strategic Objective

	GOAL	Description
FINANCIAL and MARKET	Target markets	
	Product range	
	Sales volume and profitability for the planned period	
	Comparative growth expectations	
	Countries to operate in	
	Regional concentration	
	Strategic partnerships considered	
OPERATIONAL/PERSONNEL/ MANAGEMENT	Organization	
	Training and experience	
	Wage and compensation	
	Investment goals	
	Labor turnover rate	

(*Continued*)

	GOAL	Description
	Safety regulations	
	Environmental standards	
	Technology and equipment choice	
	Scrap rates	
	Maintenance and repair policies	
	Product standards	
	Long-term capacity plans	
	Production quantities	
	Labor level	
	Inventory level	
	Overtime work	
	Subcontractor	

IMECO - SSP - OG1

Components of Strategy

Prepared by: _____.   Business:_____.

Authorized by: _____.   Project: _____ Date: _____.

		MARKET	
		NEW	**EXISTING**
PRODUCT	**NEW**	DIVERSIFICATION	PRODUCT DEVELOPMENT
	EXISTING	MARKET DEVELOPMENT	MARKET PENETRATION

SSP – CS1

Generic Competitive Strategies

Prepared by: _____. Business: _____.

Authorized by: _____. Project: _____ Date: _____.

COMPETITIVE ADVANTAGE	
COST	**DIFFERENTIATION**

		COST	DIFFERENTIATION
SCOPE	**BROAD**	COST LEADERSHIP	DIFFERENTIATION
	NARROW	COST FOCUSING	DIFFERENTIATION FOCUSING

SSP – GS1

REAL BUSINESS CASES IN STRATEGIC PLANNING

All the strategic planning workshop projects issued in the following chapters are related to the real-world organizations (listed below) that are from a variety of industry. All the data and information that is used and presented in the following chapters is real.

Organizations:

- Logistics Co.
- Packaging Machine Manufacturer
- Electronics Support Services Co.
- Metal Packaging Group
- Information Bureaus
- Plastics Packaging Co.
- Port Management
- Tube Packaging Co.
- Vocational Training Organization
- Building Materials Producer
- Application Service Provider

The workshops were geared toward developing the organization's strategic plans for the next five years. The objective was to:

- identify the developments and trends in macroeconomic factors that affect the industry most;

DOI: 10.4324/9781003519614-8

- understand the most influential forces in the industry (customers, suppliers, competitors, related public agencies and organizations, lenders, etc.) and project the positive and negative scenarios to be created by these forces;
- ascertain the institution's competitive advantages, success factors and key weaknesses;
- identify the potential opportunities, strategic objective, primary goals and related key strategies of the institution.

"Brainstorming" and "Workshop" approaches were used in addition to the Systematic Strategic Planning (SSP) methodology throughout the work.

Though for the majority of the organizations, the pattern of the simplified version of SSP methodology and its techniques were used, for some only the pattern but not the recommended techniques were applied.

Participants included senior managers and related staff from the institution as well as experienced people from the institution and related parties (stakeholders, suppliers, customer representatives, sector representatives, associations, related public agencies and organizations, etc.). Most of the time, the number of participants in parallel group work sessions was around 12–20. The moderator managed the workshops and brainstorming sessions, in five working days, mainly according to the working topics specified below.

Working Topics of the Workshops:

- Organization Description
- Environmental Analysis
  - *Macroeconomic Analysis*
  - *Analysis of Industry Forces*
- Trends Affecting the Sector
- Positive/Negative Scenarios
  - *Positive Scenarios*
  - *Negative Scenarios*
- Evolution of the Organization
- Current Status of the Organization
  - *Strengths & Weaknesses*
  - *Competitive Advantages, Success Factors, Key Vulnerabilities*
- Future Design of the Organization
  - *Organization Opportunity Definition*
  - *Strategic Objective*
  - *Main Goals*
  - *Main Strategies*

Chapter 7

Logistics Co.

Company provides logistics services to different sectors such as automotive, iron and steel, cement, ready-mixed concrete, hazardous materials, chemicals, agro-agriculture, textile, retail, food, telecommunications and FMCG. It also provides many services such as road, sea, air, railway transportation, free and bonded warehouse management, micro-distribution, project transportation, home and office logistics, customs clearance and insurance services at home and abroad.

Environmental Analysis

The effects of external factors such as market dynamics, customer expectations, competitive conditions, strategies and objectives of competitors, suppliers, substitutes on the logistics sector for the next five years were reviewed in brainstorming and group study sessions and the following results were obtained:

Analysis of Industry Forces

The forces that most influence a business are the groups that makeup competition within the industry in which it operates:

- Competition between companies involved in the industry
- The threat of potential new firms
- Customers' bargaining power

DOI: 10.4324/9781003519614-9

- The threat of substitute products
- The power of suppliers
- Other interest profits (government, trade associations, financiers, etc.)

The effectiveness of these forces determines the intensity of competition in an industry.

This analysis was carried out by different working groups. It shows the summary status of the effects of the competitive forces in the industry on the sector of the analysis results formed from the perspectives of different working groups.

Rivalry:

- The number of active companies (warehouse and distribution) is a maximum of 30–35. The number is low. Competition in local companies is high and the number is high.
- Growth is rapid.
- The variety of services is similar.
- Fixed expenses are high.
- Exit costs from the sector are high.

* *Competition is high.*

New Players:

- There are brand organizations.
- Investment costs are high to take part in the sector.
- The sector is at the beginning of the life cycle, in the learning phase.
- There are problems in accessing distribution channels.
- There are legal restrictions, regulations. But its follow-up is not smooth.
- Scale size (growth) reduces costs.
- There may be acquisitions and/or mergers.

* *International companies in logistics are likely to enter to this field.*

Customers:

- There is the possibility of alternative supply for customers. Changing suppliers in the warehouse is costly, but not in distribution.
- Price-driven:
  In addition to the classic service, they expect optimization that is efficient and reduces operational costs.

They are also ready to share the rewards of this return. However, there is a lower cost expectation of contracts.

- Core customers have the power to influence the industry.
- Customers can also carry out their own logistics activities (high bargaining power for distribution, but not for the warehouse.)
- E-commerce substitution can pose a threat.
- The impact on the activities of the sectors served is many.

* *The customer is decisive.*

Suppliers:

- There are direct and indirect suppliers:
  Direct supply: In the use of external warehouses.
  Indirect procurement: In the use of people, equipment, vehicles, software and consumables.
- For direct supply:
  No limits. Accessible.
  Their services are not unique.
  They can become competitors.
  For them, logistics firms have great potential.

Trends Affecting the Sector

Along with the above industry analysis results, we also reviewed the trends of macroeconomic external factors such as demographic, economic, legal-political, technological and social changes to the logistics sector over the next five years, in brainstorming sessions, and the following conclusions were obtained:

- The effect of the population growth rate on the growth of the sector is positive.
- The focus on the Marmara region will be continued.
- Population growth in major cities will continue.
- Where there is population growth, distribution logistics will improve.
- The impact of developments in neighboring countries will be positive.
- The Aegean region will gain importance in terms of agricultural activities.
- The speed of logistics investments in developing regions will be greater than the speed of investment in developed regions.

- Developments in e-commerce and employment will increase the need for distribution channels and distribution channels will expand.
- Depending on consumption, the number of regional distribution centers will increase.
- The impact of the diversification of education-related needs on the sector will be positive.
- With the increase in the level of education, better quality employment will be provided.
- Wages will fall with the supply-demand balance due to the increase in the number of educated people.
- Reverse logistics will increase.
- Due to the increase in the number of trained qualified people, it will be difficult to find blue-collar employees.
- An increase in GNP has a lot of impact.
- Improvement of income distribution has positive effects (the purchasing power of people increases and accelerates consumption.)
- The decline in the income of the elderly will adversely affect it.
- The increase in the income of young people will have a positive effect.
- The impact of a decline in inflation would be positive.
- It will be negative, as the number of investments will decrease.
- The impact of new legal regulations will be positive.
- The impact will be negative as the unemployment rate will increase.
- The increase in unemployment will ensure that quality employees in the sector are available at less cost.
- Since the distortion of income distribution increases the possibility of large company growth (outsourcing), the effect will be positive.
- The depreciation of the Turkish Lira has a positive impact on the sector.
- Stabilization is not disturbed.
- Oil prices are adversely affected, input costs increase and the overall impact is negative.
- An increase in the personal debt ratio has no effect.
- Credibility will reflect positively on the domestic borrowing ratio, and accordingly, the contribution to the sector will be positive.
- The increase in domestic debt may bring about an economic crisis.
- Competition regulations adversely affect.
- Commercial laws (labor and worker safety, labor laws) have a negative impact.
- The effect of the regulations is positive. The definitions and practices of the sector become clear.

- If the reflection of the laws does not affect the companies under the stairs, the sector will be adversely affected.
- Incentives will increase and its impact on employment and costs will be positive.
- Environmental regulations will be positive for companies that are sensitive to this issue and have completed their investment.
- Environmental regulations will be negative as they will increase investment costs.
- Recycling will increase reverse logistics opportunities.
- Political stabilization continues.
- There may be a possibility of a government coalition. The effect is negative.
- The impact of the presidency and the federal structure will be positive, as it will lead to an increase in vitality, mobility and investment.
- Negative social mobility adversely affects the sector.
- The impact of technology on daily consumption understanding and habits is positive, however costs may increase.
- Regional developments can have a positive impact.
- The increase in the number of households has a positive effect.
- Individuality positively affects.
- The income and consumption of the conservative people have increased and will increase. The effect is positive.
- Product diversity provides a positive effect on the sector.
- The track of technology is poor. Its use and follow-up should be at world standards.
- Manpower is cheap and there will still be no need for technology.
- Companies that make technological investments will grow faster and the sector will be positively affected.
- Rising standards in the industry will necessitate technological investments.
- The industry needs differentiation (technological innovations).
- Innovation, technology will make a difference.
- Hidden costs reduce the profit margin. Innovation and the use of technology must increase.
- R&D spending will increase.
- It needs automation.
- Standardization, product diversity, cost, competition factors and the increase in domestic opportunities can also pave the way for investments in this direction (cheap domestic supply.)

- The management of service diversity from a single source is desired. The effect of companies reaching this level of competence is positive.
- There will be more outsourcing opportunities. Only companies that are interested in their field of activity will take decisions in this direction and implement them.
- In addition to classical logistics services, consultancy requests may come from customers.
- Factors that create added value for the sector to deliver the right goods to the right place at the right time, give expertise and cost advantage, give the chance to catch up with sales, contribute to the formation of new markets, eliminate logistics investment costs.
- Customer, regardless of the sector, is anyone who needs transportation and warehouse.
- Sector segmentation varies according to scale, location, spot or contract, importers, domestic/local companies and service types.
- Success factors; technological infrastructure, innovation, commitment, human resources (HR), service diversity, awareness, financial structure, references.
- Exit from the sector does not increase (e.g., bankruptcy, leaving). Entering to sector requires long-term investments.
- Company marriages began. Small companies are interested in global-scale companies.
- Fluctuations are high throughout the year and month.
- Sector turnover (80%) is accounted for by 20% of the logistics companies.
- Has the development of the sector been completed?
  - Trained human resources are insufficient.
  - There are things to be learned from multinationals.
  - The costs are not at the required level.
  - The standard of service is not at the desired level.
  - The truck market is insufficient.

Positive/Negative Scenarios

The potential positive and negative scenarios for the logistics sector over the next five years are set out in the following definitions, as a result of group work, taking into account the above-mentioned worldwide and nationwide significant developments in the sector.

Positive Scenarios

- The use of e-commerce will become widespread and the sector will grow.
- Growth in the economy will positively affect the sector.
- Growing need to outsource.
- The need will increase in the eastern regions of Turkey, the Middle Eastern market, the Turkic Republics and North Africa.
- Sector aims to highly educated-level employees, institutionalization, quality and service diversity.
- Increased investments in training, operational efficiency and technology will reduce customer costs.
- Increase in the reverse logistics service.

Negative Scenarios

- Real costs will rise.
- Political instability.
- Legal obligations.
- Market entry of global logistics companies.
- E-commerce and service diversity will lead to uncertainty and losses.
- It will be difficult to find qualified employees.
- Customer behavior will be price-oriented.

Positive Scenario Definitions

- As a result of the increase in need in the eastern regions of Turkey, the Middle East market, the Turkic Republics and North Africa, the level of education, institutionalization, quality and the orientation toward service diversity will also increase in the sector.
- Depending on the positive outcome of the politics, the need for return from the eastern and southeastern provinces will increase and will provide added value to the sector.
- The growth in the economy will also enable the growth of the companies that are/will be our customers, which will increase the use of outsourcing in the logistical sense.
- The widespread use of e-commerce will lead to an increase in reverse logistics services and diversify distribution channels.

■ As a result of the growth in the economy and the investments to be made by foreign-origin companies in the country, outsource services will increase.
■ The growth in the economy and the spread of e-commerce will lead to an increase in the demand for outsourcing and reverse logistics.
■ The increase in the level of education and the development of technology will provide specialization in products and services.

Current Status of the Organization

Considering the stages of the enterprise from past to present, the following results were obtained through brainstorming and group studies in order to determine the strengths and weaknesses they have created in the business structure. In addition, the strengths and weaknesses of the organization are compared with the skills of the main competitors to determine their competitive advantage.

Strengths and Weaknesses

Table 7.1 shows the internal analysis with a functional approach. In this study, internal factors such as workforce, technology, organization and management, operational issues, products and market positions, financial characteristics, etc. are taken into consideration. The table shows:

■ strengths as (+),
■ weaknesses as (–).

Competitive Advantages, Success Factors, Key Vulnerabilities

Table 7.2 is a comparison table with the main competitors that results in the firm's competitive advantages, success factors, and weaknesses. In short, we can say the following (Table 7.2):

■ Competitive advantages – factors that give the business an advantage over its competitors and key factors on which the strategy of the business will be formed.

Table 7.1 Internal Analysis Table

	Factors	Strengths/ Weaknesses
Marketing	Firm's products/services; breadth of product line	+
	Concentration of sales in a few products or to a few customers	−
	Ability to gather needed information about markets	−
	Market share or submarket shares	−
	Product/service mix and expansion potential	+
	Channels of distribution: number, coverage and control	−
	Effective sales organization	−
	Product/service image, reputation and quality	+
	Imaginative, efficient and effective sales promotion and advertising	−
	Pricing strategy and pricing flexibility	+
	Procedures for digesting market feedback and developing new products, services or markets	−
	After-sale service and follow up	+
	Goodwill/brand loyalty	+
Finance and Accounting	Ability to raise short-term capital	−
	Ability to raise long-term capital: debt/equity	+
	Corporate-level resources	+
	Cost of capital relative to industry and competitors	+
	Tax considerations	−
	Relations with owners, investors and stockholders	+
	Leverage positions	+
	Cost of entry and barriers to entry	−
	Price-earnings ratio	−
	Working capital; flexibility of capital structure	+
	Effective cost control, ability to reduce costs	−
	Financial size	−
	Efficient and effective accounting system for cost, budget and profit planning	−

(Continued)

Table 7.1   Internal Analysis Table (*Continued*)

	Factors	Strengths/Weaknesses
Production/Operations Technical	Raw materials cost and availability	+
	Inventory control systems; inventory turnover	−
	Location of facilities; layout and utilization of facilities	−
	Economies of scale	−
	Technical efficiency of facilities and utilization of capacity	+/−
	Effective use of subcontracting	−
	Degree of vertical integration, value added and profit margin	−
	Efficiency and cost/benefit of equipment	?
	Effective operation control procedures	
	Cost and technological competencies relative to industry and competitors	−
	Research and development/technology/innovation	−
	Patents, trademarks and similar legal protection	N/A
Personnel	Management personnel	−
	Employees' skill and morale	?
	Labor relations cost compared to industry and competition	−
	Efficient and effective personnel policies	−
	Effective use of incentives to motivate performance	−
	Ability to level peaks and valleys of employment	?
	Employee turnover and absenteeism	−
	Specialized skills	+
	Experience	+
Organization of General Management	Organizational structure	+
	Firm's image and prestige	+
	Firm's record for achieving objectives	+
	Organization of communication system	+
	Overall organizational control system	+
	Organizational climate, culture	+
	Use of systematic procedures and techniques in decision making	?
	Top-management skill, capacities and interest	?
	Strategic planning system	−
	Intraorganizational synergy	

Table 7.2   Competitive Advantages, Success Factors, Vulnerabilities Table

	Factors	Log. Co.	Comp. X	C. A.	S. F.	W. F.
Marketing	Firm's products/services; breadth of product line	+	+	☐	☒	☐
	Concentration of sales in a few products or to a few customers	−	+	☐	☐	☒
	Ability to gather needed information about markets	−	+	☐	☐	☒
	Market share or submarket shares	−	+	☐	☐	☒
	Product/service mix and expansion potential	+	+	☐	☒	☐
	Channels of distribution: number, coverage and control	−	+	☐	☐	☒
	Effective sales organization	−	+	☐	☐	☒
	Service image, reputation and quality	+	+	☐	☒	☐
	Imaginative, efficient and effective sales promotion and advertising	−	+	☐	☐	☒
	Pricing strategy and pricing flexibility	+	+	☐	☒	☐
	Procedures for digesting market feedback and developing new products, services or markets	+	+	☐	☒	☐
	After-sale service and follow up	+	+	☐	☒	☐
	Goodwill/brand loyalty	+	+	☐	☒	☐
Finance and Accuonting	Ability to raise short-term capital	−	−	☐	☐	☐
	Ability to raise long-term capital: debt/ equity	+	+	☐	☒	☐
	Corporate-level resources	+	+	☐	☒	☐
	Cost of capital relative to industry and competitors	+	−	☐	☒	☐
	Tax considerations	−	+	☐	☐	☐
	Relations with owners, investors and stockholders	+	+	☐	☒	☐
	Leverage positions	+		☐	☐	☐
	Cost of entry and barriers to entry	+	+	☐	☒	☐
	Price-earnings ratio	−	−	☐	☐	☐
	Working capital; flexibility of capital structure	+	−	☒	☐	☐
	Effective cost control, ability to reduce costs	−	+	☐	☐	☒
	Financial size	−	+	☐	☐	☒
	Efficient and effective accounting system for cost, budget and profit planning	−	+	☐	☐	☒

(Continued)

Table 7.2 Competitive Advantages, Success Factors, Vulnerabilities Table (*Continued*)

	Factors	Log. Co.	Comp. X	C. A.	S. F.	W. F.
Production/Technical	Raw materials cost and availability	+	+	□	☒	□
	Inventory control systems; inventory turnover	+	+	□	☒	□
	Location of facilities; layout and utilization	+	+	□	☒	□
	Economies of scale	−	+	□	□	☒
	Technical efficiency of facilities and utilization of capacity	"+/−"	+	□	☒	□
	Effective use of subcontracting	+	+	□	☒	□
	Degree of vertical integration, value added and profit margin	−	+	□	□	☒
	Efficiency and cost/benefit of equipment	+	+	□	☒	□
	Effective operation control procedures	−	+	□	□	☒
	Cost and technological competencies relative to industry and competitors	−	+	□	□	☒
	Research and development/technology/innovation	−	+	□	□	☒
	Patents, trademarks and similar		+	□	□	□
Personnel	Management personnel	−	+	□	□	☒
	Employees' skill and morale	+	"+/−"	□	☒	□
	Labor cost compared to industry and competition	−	+	□	□	☒
	Efficient and effective personnel policies	−	−	□	□	□
	Effective use of incentives to motivate performance	−	−	□	□	□
	Ability to level peaks and valleys of employment	−	−	□	□	□
	Employee turnover and absenteeism	−	−	□	□	□
	Specialized skills	+	+	□	☒	□
	Experience	+	+	□	☒	□
Organization of General Management	Organizational structure	−	+	□	□	☒
	Firm's image and prestige	+	+	□	☒	□
	Firm's record for achieving objectives	+	+	□	☒	□
	Organization of communication system	+	−	☒	□	□
	Overall organizational control system	+	+	□	☒	□
	Organizational climate, culture	+	+	□	☒	□
	Use of systematic procedures and techniques	−	−	□	□	☒
	Top-management skill, capacities and interest	−	+	□	□	☒
	Strategic planning system	−	+	□	□	☒
	Intraorganizational synergy	−	+	□	□	☒

- Success factors – important factors that the business must have but are also typically found in every profitable competitor. It does not constitute a potential source for any strategic advantage.
- Key vulnerabilities – factors in which the business does not currently have the necessary skills, knowledge or resources to compete effectively.

Future Design of the Organization

Opportunities for the organization (taking into account the competitive advantages of the enterprise and matching them with potential positive scenarios of the sector), and therefore the strategic objective, main goals and main strategies to be achieved over the next five years are indicated by the brainstorming and group work sessions.

Organization's Opportunity Definition

To respond to the needs of our existing and potential customers in domestic and international locations.

Strategic Objective

- Unlimited growth with our customers.
- Best service with our reliable partner.

Main Goals

Organization and Operation Goals

Organizational structure

- Independent local management – subordinate to the director of the warehouse and distribution.
- Strengthening the sales staff.
- Process improvement team.
- Appointment of industry managers.
- Group office establishment.
- IT warehouse project manager.

Education and experience

- Logistics sector experience.
- Undergraduate level.
- Minimum two years of experience.

Remuneration policy

- Performance-based bonus system.
- Charge above market average.
- Premiums and benefits according to regional conditions.
- Performance management system application for blue collar.

Investment goals

- Bursa, Istanbul (Anatolian side) new warehouse.
- Domestic hubs (Antalya, Samsun and other regions).
- Overseas real estate and equipment for rent.
- Automation investments.

Environmental standards	ISO 14001
Occupational safety standards	OHSAS 18001
Quality standards	ISO 9001, ISO 10002 (use of the same standards abroad).
Complaint level	Customer satisfaction should not fall below 75 points.
Capacity utilization	Should not fall below 75%.
Labor level	Reducing the level of labor by increasing automation.
Subcontractor use	Bringing down the subcontractor utilization rate.
Finance and Market Goals	
Target market	Priority is the sectors and countries in which our current customers are located.
Service variety • Storage • Distribution: Domestic (full scope), overseas (inter-warehouse) • Inventory management	
Sales volume	%25/year (min. %20)
Profitability (EBIT)	5% min.

Main Strategies

In the light of the opportunities and main goals identified above, and according to the "components of strategy" (Ansoff 1970), it seems appropriate that the preference of the enterprise in the product-market position should be to develop new nearby markets with existing services. Therefore, *market development* is one of the main strategies.

Market development:

- Overseas (strategic partnership and/or with our own means – primarily textile, telecommunications and automotive spare parts):
  - Bulgaria
  - Romania
  - Russia
  - Ukraine
  - Morocco
- Domestic (hubs – by our own means):
  - Samsun
  - Antalya
  - Antep
  - Kayseri
  - Erzurum
- Warehouse, distribution and inventory management – by our own means.
- To establish a new warehouse on the Anatolian side.
- Warehouse for rent in Bursa.

According to "general competitive strategies" (Porter 1998), differentiation seems to be the most basic competitive advantage that an enterprise can have, and a narrower scope rather than global as a field of activity seems appropriate. Therefore, the *service differentiation focusing* is another of its main strategies.

Service differentiation focusing:

- Joint venture with a company from abroad in inventory management.
- ASR storage and distribution (Turkish market.)
- Standardization of automation systems for the retail industry.

Chapter 8

Packaging Machine Manufacturer (PMM)

The company is in an ambitious position in the production of packaging machinery and equipment (using the appropriate method and technology) which produces non-ordinary plastic bags and packaging products that people may need at an affordable level.

Environmental Analysis

The effects of external factors such as demographic, economic, legal-political, technological and social changes, market dynamics, customer expectations, competitive conditions, strategies and objectives of competitors, suppliers, substitutes on the packaging machinery production sector over the next five years were reviewed in brainstorming sessions:

- Especially developed countries are abandoning machine production due to the high cost of labor and environmental pollution. Instead, they sell technology and raw materials. Production is therefore shifting to underdeveloped countries such as Turkey.
- The importance given to quality has increased in the surrounding countries. Companies that produce quality machinery and create a good service network have a high chance. Service and brand image are important.

DOI: 10.4324/9781003519614-10

- The China-Taiwan war could wipe Taiwan out of this sector. But in the future, Taiwan may be replaced by China. This may not be an advantage for producers in Turkey.
- Taiwan is the biggest competitor in Turkey. Their manufacturers entered the sector with cheap credit lines and raw materials.
- Taiwan used to be a big competitor, but Taiwanese machines turned out to be of poor quality. Difficult times await Taiwan in the future. It is very difficult to be a competitor to a Turkish manufacturer that makes quality production like PMM.
- Taiwanese are probably investigating why their market share in the sector is falling. Taiwan should not be discarded though its market shares have fallen and its machines have become apparent as poor quality. Even if the Turkish market shrinks, they can enter the Russian market. Our biggest advantage is our geographical location.
- Most companies do not buy machines from Taiwan, as the user manual is not understood and the spare parts cannot be accessible.
- The use of plastic in the Russian market has increased a lot. In the first stage, Russia got used to the use of plastic bags, and a lot of plastic was exported. In the second stage, Russia bought machinery from Turkey for the production of plastic bags. In the third stage, the start of machine manufacturing in Russia can happen at any time.
- Thinking that the sector was promising, there were many companies that entered the market and produced poor-quality machines in order to make easy money. However, poor-quality machines damaged the Turkish image. Confidence in Turkish machines in the domestic and foreign markets is decreasing.
- The emergence of alternative products to plastic is unlikely in the short term. Perhaps in the long run there can be such an alternative. However, it should not be forgotten that all forests must be cut down even to meet the world's annual packaging needs.
- Plastic packaging and machinery are a developing sector in the world. There are two kinds of approaches in this industry. In the first approach, poor-quality goods are produced. In the second approach, quality and specific packaging and machinery are produced. Fast and efficient machines are popular in the sector. But the biggest problem in the Turkish market is the lack of serious service networks. In contrast, it is an advantage that labor is cheap and environmental laws are not seriously enforced. In order to grow, it is necessary to produce specific and high-quality machines. Those who cannot produce specific and quality machines will be cut off from the sector.

- Compared to the surrounding countries, the technology in Turkey is more advanced. Turkey is older in the market.
- Turkey's accession to the EU has a positive long-term impact on the sector. In order to compete with the world, Turkey's entry into the EU is absolutely essential.
- There is also the other side of the coin. Mandatory norms with the entry into the EU put the sector in trouble. The sector is adversely affected by the implementation of environmental laws or the reduction of production in order to reduce environmental pollution, and the withdrawal of labor wages to EU norms (which are currently low in Turkey).
- There is an expectation that sales will increase after the crisis in the sector. Positive developments can be expected with a possible economic growth after the crisis. The growth of the world economy also affects the sector positively. Oil to be found in Turkey may cause prices to fall and the cost of raw materials to decrease. The possibility of lowering taxes can also be an advantage.
- Definitely, quality and specific machines should be produced. R&D is very important.
- Market proximity, appears to be positive in the short term, and the advantages used for it (such as sending machine parts alongside passengers) may be negative in the long term with the entry into the world market.
- Producers in Turkey should apply different strategies for the surrounding countries and for the other European countries.
- Most of the negative scenarios are due to the political and economic instability in Turkey.

Trends Affecting the Sector

The trends that the effects of the factors determined in the environmental analysis will create in the packaging machinery production sector over the next five years were reviewed in brainstorming sessions and the following results were obtained:

- The biggest competitor in the sector is Taiwan.
- Taiwan produces machines of poor quality with inadequate service support, so Taiwan's influence in the sector is decreasing.
- Preparations need to be made for a second wave of Taiwan in the future.

- The support provided by Taiwan banks does not come from Turkish banks.
- The Turkish government is not providing enough support.
- The profitability rate of domestic producers is low, so opportunities are insufficient.
- The plastic packaging industry is developing around the world.
- There are two different types of machines, either quality/specific or non-quality.
- There is a demand for efficient machines in the world market.
- There is a lack of service and technical support in the Turkish market.
- Environmental laws and cheap labor are driving the demand in Turkey.
- The outsourcing approach is preferred in research and design, manufacturing and marketing fields.
- The quality expectations from outsourcing cannot always be achieved.
- Patents in Turkey do not provide adequate protection.
- There are not enough blue- and white-collar plastics experts in Turkey and in the world.
- Raw materials and some spare parts are imported.
- Being a subcontractor to large manufacturers can be a profitable strategy.
- Russia is becoming an important market for outgoing companies.
- South America and Africa are seen as potential market areas.
- Geographical proximity is considered an advantage.
- It is foreseen that the Turkish market may expand.

Positive/Negative Scenarios

The potential positive and negative scenarios for the packaging machinery production sector over the next five years are set out in the following definitions, as a result of group works, taking into account the above-mentioned worldwide and nationwide significant developments in the sector.

Positive Scenarios

- The lack of production in this sector in the surrounding countries and accordingly there is a necessity for market development.

- In developed countries, especially as a result of EU policies, there is a decrease in production in the packaging sector and the production shifts to countries like Turkey.
- Increasing selectivity and demand for quality products in surrounding countries.
- Falling oil prices and the discovery of oil in Turkey.
- Increasing rate of production of plastics in Russia and the demand for purchasing plastics machinery by Russian producers.
- Providing incentives and loans to third-world countries.
- Government defines the sector as an area with high added value and accordingly increases its support.

Negative Scenarios

- Increasing number of manufacturers leads to image damage and reduces confidence in Turkish machinery.
- Similar occurrences, such as the Iraq war, may create stagnation in the sector.
- Regulations such as environmental sensitivity, etc. may trigger the escape from the sector.
- High possibility of natural disasters.
- Russia can produce machinery and/or purchase equipment from countries other than Turkey.
- The burdens of the EU process.
- Falling behind in competition due to failure to ensure the norms of conformity to the world market.
- The contraction of the sector is a result of the decline of oil and other natural resources and the emergence of alternative products to plastic.

Evolution of the Organization

87:
Established date.
3 partners

88:
Being subcontractor of the company X.
Start keeping accounting records.

89:
Change of shareholding structure.
Separation from X.
Being in electronic repair.
Exporting.

90:
The first independent order was received.
Initial investment (purchase of lathe and welding machine).
The first design is made with chalk on the wall.
2 staff

92:
Start of institutionalization.
Receiving orders for 40 machines.
Design of a new machine that does not exist in Turkey.
Discovering and patenting plastic that disappears in nature.
Transition to plastic production.
Continue exporting.

93:
Delivery of 40 machines.
Growth of exports.
Start of outsourcing.
Making a specialized machine that makes rustling bags.
Buying a 300 m² place.

94:
Delivery of the first 3 orders received.
Export of reinforced bag making machine.
First export to Saudi Arabia.

95:
Number of staff 20.
Developing an organizational structure.
Spending a lot of money on R&D.

96:
Entering the Romanian market.
Starting of Greece, Czech Republic, Bulgaria, Russia and Macedonia exports.

The construction of a large and special machine.
Construction of a trio of specialized machines.
Issuing Israeli representation.

97:
Moving to a big place.
Fair in Tüyap.
Continuation of R&D investments.
Staff 25 people.
Professionalization of the administrative structure.

98:
Moving to a larger place.
Staff 30 people.
50% domestic market, 50% foreign market.
Outsourcing 20%.
Shift from the Romanian market to the Russian market.

00-02:
Transition to standardization.
Mainly exporting to Russia.
Faced up with credit risks.
$1 million turnover per year.

Current Status of the Organization

Considering the stages of the enterprise from past to present, the following results were obtained through brainstorming and group studies in order to determine the strengths and weaknesses that they have created in the business structure. In this study, internal factors such as workforce, technology, organization and management, operational issues, products and market positions, financial characteristics, etc. are taken into consideration.

■ The fact that exports are around 50% is the most important competency of PMM. This leads to a decrease in the risk distribution. However, it is important whether exports are sustainable or not. The fact that very cheap plastic bags went abroad, especially to Romania, reduced the purchase of machinery here in Turkey.

■ The most important feature of PMM is the high level of exports. In exporting, especially in the Russian market, service provision can be more important than quality. There is currently no company in Turkey that will provide such a service.

■ Customer-oriented production can be seen as negative from the PMM's point of view. That's why it's hard to go into mass production. Mass production should be started and standardization should be made.

■ It is very important to make a well-understood product description. It is also very important to determine which country to sell with which product quality. For example, a B quality machine can be sold to Algeria, Taiwan or Russia. But we can only sell an A quality machine to Germany.

■ Promotion and marketing activities should be prioritized. Promotion and marketing activities are missing in PMM, which is already the biggest problem of SMEs.

■ R&D is absolutely crucial. R&D studies should be continued without interruption.

■ In the previous years, a lot of investment has been made in R&D. The funds allocated for R&D should be used effectively and should not affect production negatively.

■ PMM's technical know-how and product development capability are much better than other SMEs in the sector. In particular, designing specific products should be considered as a great advantage.

■ PMM is a company that prepares technical drawings and manufactures with quality outsourcing. At the moment there is no such firm. However, there is a lack of institutionalization and organization in PMM. Without them, it is impossible to go any further.

■ A company with a turnover of one million dollars should move to professional staff as soon as possible.

■ Due to PMM outsourcing, it pursues a high price policy domestically, but low in real terms compared to Taiwan.

■ PMM can only orient itself to design and expand its market accordingly instead of production on its own.

■ Delivery times are very important. PMM is unable to deliver products on time and loses prestige.

■ Patent and trademark registration is very important. But even if a patent is obtained, it can be copied very easily and the machines can be sold cheaper.

Strengths

- High product development ability and being open to development.
- Quality production and customer focus.
- Export market share is 50%.
- High knowledge of management.
- Having a flexible company structure.
- Gained experience within the market.
- High technical knowledge and adequate infrastructure.
- High manufacturing quality and minimal service requirements.
- Allocation of resources for R&D and new projects.
- The presence of technical documentation.
- Desire to improve.
- Acceptance of mistakes.

Weaknesses

- Lack of institutionalization.
- The length of reaction times to customers.
- Deficiencies in promotional and marketing activities.
- R&D is not a separate department.
- Rather than being a profitable firm, working only with the spirit of engineering and entrepreneurship.
- Lack of equity.
- Inadequate financial infrastructure.
- Lack of production and operations management.
- Length of delivery times.
- The physical infrastructure of the factory.

Future Design of the Organization

In the light of the results obtained in the above studies, the strategic objective, main goals and main strategies to be achieved for the organization for the next five years is indicated by the brainstorming and group work.

Strategic Objective

To be the number one in the world in manufacturing of machinery and equipment, that produces non-ordinary plastic bags and packaging products that people may need, at an affordable level with the appropriate methods and technology and on the basis of total quality and reliability.

Main Goals

- Developing markets by providing representation and servicing rights to the countries of the CIS, Eastern Bloc, Middle East and North Africa, conducting market research in South America and other countries, and taking initiatives.
- Establishing cooperation in the field of assembly with a local company that can make appropriate investments, can provide services and sales in the targeted countries where there are possibilities of producing machinery.
- Expanding the market all over Turkey and maintaining leadership in specific production.
- Creating a unit that produces complete solutions to target countries and markets.
- Developing the organizational structure that will ensure institutionalization.
- Reaching a minimum market share of 50% in Turkey by our product range.
- Increasing the export to ten times of the current position by innovative products.
- Achieving an average annual real growth of 30% and a turnover of $9 million.
- Maintaining leadership in the neighboring countries.
- Using appropriate design technology by combining it with creativity.
- Being a pioneer in the market by designing new products.
- Starting the work of establishing a management information system that integrates production, service and administrative management.
- 25% profitability.

Main Strategies

In the light of the main goals set out above, and according to the "components of strategy" (Ansoff 1970), it seems appropriate that the preference of this entrepreneurial enterprise, which is at the introductory stage, in the product-market position is to develop new nearby markets with innovative products. Therefore, *diversification* is one of the main strategies.

According to "general competitive strategies" (Porter 1998), by knowing that innovation and differentiation as the main competitive advantages of this enterprise and focusing initially on a narrower scope as an area of marketing activity, *differentiation focusing* seems to be another appropriate strategy for this firm.

Chapter 9

Electronics Support Services, Inc.

It is a technology company that provides electronic and mechanical support services to OEM, ODM and logistics companies, regardless of brand and model. It provides brand-independent and high-volume technical support services to companies in accordance with standards such as production, after-sales repair, R&D and technical consultancy, spare parts supply and inventory management.

Trends Affecting the Sector

The effects of external factors such as demographic, economic, legal-political, technological and social changes, market dynamics, customer expectations, competitive conditions, strategies and targets of competitors, suppliers and substitutes on the technical support services sector over the next five years were reviewed in brainstorming sessions and the following results were obtained:

- The after-sales service sector will lead to the development of service understanding by integrating the maintenance and repair demand with logistics services and customer relations services.
- The expectation of the customer to adopt cost-oriented approach and to supply many services from a single source will increase.

DOI: 10.4324/9781003519614-11

■ In developed countries, the domestic demand of the sector will decrease and it will be adversely affected by the economic developments, and global brands will seek new markets and investments.

■ In the next five years, countries with increasing consumption capacity such as Brazil, Russia, India, Africa, Iran and Turkey will form the developing market.

■ The transfer of new technologies in emerging markets will increase and create new demand for services in the domestic market.

■ Global brands, in their market development strategies, will prefer to work with local suppliers to their own standards in order to minimize political and economic risks in the regions.

■ For global brands, the fact that labor is cheap in Turkey is an element of attraction.

■ Service providers have an obligation to adapt to the strategies of manufacturers.

■ The shrinkage of spare parts will make repair difficult and repair systems expensive.

■ In Turkey, the market share is growing in the Marmara, Aegean and Central Anatolia regions.

■ The increase in education and income level will increase the purchasing power and consumption needs.

■ End-user expectations will gain importance in strategy development.

■ In countries with low GNP, the risk factor should be taken into account.

■ Turkey's GNP is growing and consumption is increasing.

■ The effect of fluctuations in the exchange rate on costs should be monitored.

■ Capital accumulation in Turkey is difficult to happen.

■ Cheap labor transfer to Turkey is taking place.

■ International companies have started to buy local companies that have capital and markets.

■ The fact that inflation is falling will have a positive effect on costs.

■ The sector's need for qualified personnel is increasing.

■ Consumption expenditures are on a downward trend.

■ Incentives for the software and technology sector in Turkey are increasing.

■ Customers' expectations regarding environmental protection will be the same as European standards.

■ There will be a tendency toward recycling.

■ The transformation of R&D into a necessity will increase the need for an extra budget.

- Speed of technology change is increasing.
- The need to invest in people is increasing.
- There is a problem in finding qualified personnel.
- The quality of logistics supply is gaining importance.
- Dependence on suppliers is not high due to the availability of alternatives.
- Customs legislation imposes restrictions.
- Evolving technology will require ongoing investment.
- Know-how is a necessity.
- Know-how should not be easily copied.
- Physical investment costs are relatively low.
- In terms of physical environment and quality standards, it is not easy to form companies that can compete in Turkey and Russia.
- In Turkey, Russia, the Middle East and Africa, end consumers do not have high expectations because they do not know their rights.

Positive/Negative Scenarios

The potential positive and negative scenarios for the technical support services sector over the next five years are set out in the following definitions, as a result of group works, taking into account the above-mentioned worldwide and nationwide significant developments in the sector.

Positive Scenarios

- The service market will shift from Europe to Turkey, Russia, the Middle East and the Far East regions.
- The sector will be looking for new distribution centers and will increase the demand for logistics services in the sector.
- Establishing strategic partnerships with logistics companies in emerging markets will increase competitiveness in the service sector.
- Consumption will increase in developing countries.
- Evolving technology will expand the maintenance and repair portfolio, and new technologies will create additional demands in emerging markets.
- The customer's need to supply many services from a single source will increase the demand for on-site services.
- Due to population growth in emerging markets and the high unemployment rate, etc., the cheap labor availability will continue.

- Financial crises and current conditions in the world will turn the competitiveness in favor of local companies.
- Local companies with strong infrastructure and markets and international companies will tend to cooperate strategically.
- Regional market leadership is open for local firms.
- The service sector will need branded companies.

Negative Scenarios

- Political instability in developing regions.
- Developing technology will reduce the need for maintenance and repair services and negatively affect the profit margin.
- The increasing demand for logistics services will reduce the market share of companies in maintenance and repair services.
- In emerging markets, the interest of foreign capital in the service sector as a player will increase.
- Technology development and service diversification in the sector will increase the need for financing.

Current Status of the Organization

Considering the stages of the enterprise from past to present, the following results were obtained through brainstorming and group studies in order to determine the strengths and weaknesses that they have created in the business structure. In this study, internal factors such as workforce, technology, organization and management, operational issues, products and market positions, financial characteristics, etc. are taken into consideration. In addition, the strengths and weaknesses of the organization were compared with the capabilities of the main competitors in order to determine its competitive advantages.

Strengths

- Company prestige/positive references.
- Entrepreneurial firm features.
- Management team that takes responsibility.
- Flexible relationships.
- Organizational climate and culture.
- Continuity in the organization.
- Skills and morale of employees.

- The ability to keep employee turnover at the same level.
- Qualified skills.
- Organization open to career development.
- Experience.
- Raw material cost and availability and supplier relations.
- R&D/Technology/Innovations
- The company's products/services quality and variety.
- Customer-focused sales.
- After-sales service and follow-up.
- Company value/brand loyalty.
- The capability to create short-term capital.
- Long-term capital generation capability.
- High credibility.
- High current ratio.

Weaknesses

- Organizational structure.
- Inefficient general organizational communication and control system.
- Disuse of systematic procedures and techniques in decision-making mechanisms.
- Senior management skills and capacities.
- Lack of strategic planning system.
- Quick change of decisions.
- Ineffective use of performance-enhancing incentives.
- Inventory control system.
- Layout of the facility.
- Technical inefficiency and utilization capacity of the plant.
- Inefficiency and cost-benefit study of equipment.
- Ineffective operational control procedures: design, planning, procurement and quality control.
- Lack of patent, trademark and similar legal protections.
- Disability to gather the information needed about the markets.
- Ineffective sales promotion.
- Intensive work with specific clients.
- Ineffective sales organization.
- Pricing strategy and inflexibility.
- Disability to take advantage of alternative financing.
- Ineffective cost control and disability to reduce costs.
- Ineffective and inefficient accounting system.

Competitive Advantages

The competitive advantages of the company, which are found by the comparison with the main competitors, are the key factors that give the business an advantage over its competitors and will be the basis for the creation of the strategy of the business.

- Entrepreneurial firm features.
- Management team that takes responsibility.
- Flexible relationships.
- Raw material cost and availability and supplier relations.
- R&D/Technology/Innovations
- The company's products/services quality and variety.

Future Design of the Organization

Opportunities for the organization (taking into account the competitive advantages of the enterprise and matching them with potential positive scenarios of the sector), and therefore the main goals and strategies to be achieved over the next five years are indicated by the brainstorming and group work sessions.

Organization's Opportunity Definition

To turn the possibility and attractiveness of market leadership and branding in the service sector into an opportunity by developing business models integrated with logistics services, providing strategic collaborations with international companies and strengthening technological infrastructure diversification in developing regions.

Main Goals

Market and Service Goals:

- Targeting leading customers in developing countries with the existing products/services variety.
- Maintenance and repair services (electronic and electro-mechanical products).

- Logistics services (distribution and warehousing).
- Customer services (call center, collection center, and database management).

Investment Goals:

- The Istanbul service location will be relocated and the electronic laboratory will be strengthened.
- Izmir service location layout will be renewed.
- In Russia, the electronic laboratory will be strengthened.
- A new service location will be opened in the Middle East and Africa region.
- Information processing and data management infrastructure will be strengthened.
- The global branding process will be accelerated.
- Customer service will be strengthened.
- There will be changes in company structures.
- R&D will be developed.

Operational and Organizational Goals:

- Define the global branding process.
- Creating a strong and sustainable organizational structure.
- Use of systems required to become a world-class organization.
- To develop a performance-based corporate culture.
- Formation of the management team.
- To increase management skills.
- To develop the talents of employees.
- To ensure synergy and unity within the organization.
- To be able to control costs effectively.
- Cost improvement.
- To improve marketing activities.
- Creating an effective sales organization.
- Efficiency.
- Development of R&D studies.

Main Strategies

In the light of the opportunities and main goals identified above, and according to the "components of strategy" (Ansoff 1970), it seems appropriate that the preference of the enterprise in the product-market position should be to develop new nearby markets (such as the Middle East) with existing services. Therefore, *market development* is one of the main strategies. On the other hand, it seems appropriate to develop existing markets (such as Turkey and Russia) with existing services. That is, for these markets, *market concentration* strategy is preferred.

Chapter 10

Metal Packaging Group

The organization was founded in 1955 with the aim of developing unique packaging solutions that would contribute to the commercial success of its customers. In 1957, the company established its first factory that produced slugs and aluminum tubes. The company, which renews its production lines with advanced technologies by incorporating technical competencies such as aluminum Monoblock aerosol can production, aluminum barrier laminated tube production, plastic barrier laminated tube production, serves global and local customers in the pharmaceutical, personal care, cosmetics, home care, food and chemical/stationery sectors with its high production capacity.

Environmental Analysis

The effects of external factors such as demographic, economic, legal-political, technological and social changes, market dynamics, customer expectations, competitive conditions, strategies and targets of competitors, suppliers and substitutes on the metal packaging production sector for the next five years were reviewed in brainstorming and group study sessions and the following results were obtained.

Macroeconomic Analysis

Macroeconomic variables affect enterprises and the industries in which they are functioning and are not under the control of the enterprises.

DOI: 10.4324/9781003519614-12

Macroeconomic variables:

■ Demographical
■ Economical
■ Legal-political
■ Technological
■ Social-cultural

This analysis should be carried out first in relation to the global and then to the region and the country. The aim is to find out the effects of macroeconomic variables on the sector, from the perspectives of different stakeholders.

This analysis was carried out by different stakeholders such as customers, suppliers, shareholders and employees gathered in different working groups. Table 10.1 shows the summary status of the effects of macroeconomic variables on the sector of the analysis results from the perspectives of different working groups. Sector with macroeconomic variable effect;

■ will be in a better state than it is now, marked as +,
■ if it will remain unchanged, blank or marked as 0,
■ if it will be in a worse state than it is now, marked as −.

Table 10.1   Macroeconomic Analysis

	Demographic					Economic								Legal-Political						Technological						Socio-Cultural			
	Population growth	Age pattern	Immigration trends	Birth and death ratios	Education level	Change in GDP	Income distribution	Interest rates	Supply of cash	Inflation rate	Unemployment rate	Foreign exchange policy	Saving&consuming trends	Tax laws	Antitrust law	Incentives	Green laws	Business law	Political stability	R&D expenditures	Innovation opportunities	New products	Acceleration - tech. change	Fastness product supply	Increase in automation	Changes in life styles	Expectancy for career	Change in family structure	Changes in personal values
Customer	0	0	+	0	+	+	+	0	−	−	−	−	−	−	−	+	+	+	−	+	+	+	+	+	+	+	0	+	0
Employees 1	+	0	+	+	+	+	+	−	−	−	−	−	−	−	−	+	−	+	−	+	+	+	+	−	+	+	0	0	0
Financor																													
Supplier	+	+	+	+	+	−	−	−	−	−	−	0	+	0	0	0	−	0	−	+	+	+	+	−	+	+	0	+	+
Shareholder	+	+	0	0	+	+	0	−	−	−	0	0	+	0	0	+	−	+	−	0	+	+	−	0	0	+	+	+	0
Employees 2	+	+	0	+	+	+	0	−	−	−	−	−	+	0	−	0	−	−	0	+	+	+	+	−	+	+	+	0	0
Result	+	+	+	+	+	+	+	−	−	−	−	?	?	−	0	+	−	+	−	+	+	+	+	0	+	+	0	+	0

+	Better
0	Not changing
−	Worse

Variables that Transform the Industry for the Better:

- Population growth rate
- Age distribution
- Migration trend
- Birth and death rate
- Education level
- Change in GNP
- Income distribution
- Incentives
- Commercial law
- R&D expenses
- Opportunities for innovation
- The pace of technological change
- Increased productivity through automation
- Change in lifestyle
- Change in family structure

Variables that do not Affect the Change of the Industry:

- Competition laws
- Product changeover rate
- Change in personal values and beliefs

Variables that Make the Industry Worse:

- Interest rates
- Money supply
- Inflation rate
- Unemployment rate
- Tax laws
- Environmental protection laws
- Political stability

Analysis of Industry Forces

The forces that most influence a business are the groups that makeup competition within the industry in which it operates:

- Competition between companies involved in the industry
- The threat of potential new firms

■ Customers' bargaining power
■ The threat of substitute products
■ The power of suppliers
■ Other interest groups (government, trade associations, financiers, etc.)

The effectiveness of these forces determines the intensity of competition in an industry.

This analysis was carried out by different working groups. Table 10.2 shows the summary status of the effects of the competitive forces on the industry, which were formed from the perspectives of the different working

Table 10.2 Analysis of Industry Forces

	Companies in the Industry					Threat of New Companies						Bargaining Power of Customers						Suppliers Bargaining Power				
	Quantity of firms in the industry	Growth rate of the industry	Differences and the specialties of the products	Fixed costs	Cost to leave the industry	Costs of the companies in the industry related with the company size	Firms which have the customer-firm loyalty	The equity needed to enter the industry	Ability to reach channel of distribution	Cost advantage related with experience	Barriers to enter the industry	The share of the customer in the whole sale	Potential of production of the products by integration	Alternative suppliers	Cost of the change of the suppliers	Flexibility in the prices	The importance of the product for the customers	Quantity of firms in the industry and the production place	Unique products sale	Substitute goods in the market	Potential of production of the products by integration	The share of the sale of the supplier
High			√	√	√						√	√										
Normal	√	√					√							√	√	√		√		√		√
Low						√		√		√			√				√		√		√	

groups' analysis. Every force has been evaluated in terms of whether it makes the sector attractive;

- high,
- normal,
- low.

Rivalry:

- The number of active companies is at a normal level. The ratio of supply and demand to each other is thought to be balanced.
- The growth rate is in a normal course.
- Product varieties and differences are high.
- Fixed expenses are high.
- Exit costs from the sector are high.

* *Competition is balanced.*

New Players:

- There are brand organizations.
- Investment costs and equity capital are high in order to take part in the sector.
- Experience in the sector is an important deterrent.
- Customer loyalty is at a normal level.
- Legal restrictions, regulations are not restrictive.
- Scale size (growth) costs don't make a big impact.
- There may be acquisitions and/or mergers.

* *Multinationals are likely to enter this field.*

Customers:

- There is the possibility of alternative supply for customers.
- The cost of supplier replacement is not very much of a factor.
- Price quality expectation in the sector is directly proportional.
- Core customers have the power to influence the industry.
- Customers are low in their ability to carry out manufacturing activities.

* *The customer is decisive.*

Suppliers:

- No limits. Accessible.
- Their products are not unique.
- They do not have a monopolistic effect on volume.
- They don't become competitors.

* Suppliers are not influential.

Positive/Negative Scenarios

The potential positive and negative scenarios for the metal packaging production sector over the next five years are set out in the following definitions, as a result of group works, taking into account the significant developments in the sector worldwide and nationwide mentioned above.

Positive Scenarios

- In the next five years, the growth in the world economy will continue slightly. Its positive effect due to the demographic factors will increase the consumption of packaging products and therefore the metal packaging.
- The difficulty of entering the sector will continue in the next five years. Experience will remain an important factor. Additionally, as customer loyalty is persistent, the shares of existing companies will increase. Improving automation will increase the profit margin as well as reduce the cost of production. Government incentives for R&D will increase. Laws that prevent unfair competition will positively affect the sector.
- Assuming that the investments will be supported by incentives, it will be attractive for existing players to invest. As a result of these investments, it will be encouraging to develop product varieties and differences. These opportunities will trigger the growth in the sector.
- The fact that supplier dependence in the sector is very high and at the same time the cost of supplier change is not very influential and therefore the positive effect of this situation on production costs will

support growth. In this way, responding to the demands of customers, who are decisive in the sector, will be possible.

■ Assuming that the income level will increase, we think that the consumption of metal-packaged products will follow an increasing trend. Since the probability of new players entering this sector is low, existing companies in the sector will be positively affected by this growth.

■ From an economic point of view, the increase in GNP globally, the change in lifestyle and family structure and the expected increase in the level of welfare will positively affect the sector.

■ Due to the balanced supply-demand structure in the sector and the continuation of growth plus the high cost of equity and investment and the low probability of new players entering the market, it is foreseen that existing players will increase their investments.

■ The entry of international companies into the sector strengthens suppliers and helps them to produce cheaper. Those who can maintain their existence can adjust their standards to the new market, for those who can't, acquisitions and mergers may occur. Competitive conditions may cause the education levels to be strengthened and the sector to continue quality production.

Negative Scenarios

■ In the next five years in the global – metal packaging sector, the uncertainties of the world economy, political instability and social conflicts, the increase in interest rates and the deterioration of macroeconomic indicators such as unemployment will have a negative impact on the sector and investment decisions. Since the economies of the countries will deteriorate, the countries will take tax measures to prevent luxury consumption and imported inputs.

■ Globally, environmental awareness is increasing day by day. Therefore, costs will increase and profitability will decrease, and there may be a contraction in the sector due to the transition to other alternative packaging materials.

■ The shrinkage of the sector is a result of the preference for different packages instead of existing packages and the availability of cheaper alternative products instead of metal packaging.

■ The money supply will shrink. This situation will cause interest rates to increase and unemployment to increase. The customer will not be able to pay for the quality.

■ The market shares of global players in the sector will increase with acquisitions, disrupting the balanced market environment.
■ Intense price and service pressure (quality expectations, deadlines, etc.) from customers will reduce the profits of companies in the sector.

Current Status of the Organization

Considering the stages of the enterprise from past to present, the following results regarding the strengths and weaknesses they have created in the business structure were obtained through brainstorming and group studies. In addition, the strengths of the organization were compared with the strengths of the main competitors to determine its competitive advantages.

Strengths and Weaknesses

Table 10.3 shows the internal analysis due to the functional approach. In this study, internal factors such as workforce, technology, organization and management, operational issues, products and market positions, financial characteristics, etc. were taken into consideration. In the table;

■ strengths shown as (+),
■ and weaknesses shown as (−).

Competitive Advantages, Success Factors, Key Vulnerabilities

Table 10.4 is a comparison table with major competitors that results in the firm's competitive advantages, success factors and weaknesses. In short, we can say the following (Table 10.5):

■ Competitive advantages – factors providing the business with an edge compared to its competitors, and therefore key factors around which to build the business strategy.
■ Success factors – factors that are important capabilities for the business to have but are also typical of every viable competitor. Does not represent a potential source of any strategic advantage.
■ Key vulnerabilities – factors on which the business currently lacks the necessary skill, knowledge, or resources to compete effectively.

Table 10.3 Internal Analysis

	Factors	Strengths/ Weaknesses
Marketing	Firm's products/services; breadth of product line	+
	Concentration of sales in a few products or to a few customers	−
	Ability to gather needed information about markets	+
	Market share or submarket shares	+
	Product/service mix and expansion potential	+
	Channels of distribution: number, coverage and control	NA
	Effective sales organization	+
	Product/service image, reputation and quality	+
	Imaginative, efficient and effective sales promotion and advertising	−
	Pricing strategy and pricing flexibility	+/−
	Procedures for digesting market feedback and developing new products, services or markets	−
	After-sale service and follow-up	+
	Goodwill/brand loyalty	+
Finance and Accounting	Ability to raise short-term capital	+
	Ability to raise long-term capital: debt/equity	+
	Corporate-level resources	+
	Cost of capital relative to industry and competitors	−
	Tax considerations	+
	Relations with owners, investors and stockholders	+
	Leverage positions	+
	Cost of entry and barriers to entry	+
	Price-earnings ratio	+
	Working capital; flexibility of capital structure	+
	Effective cost control, ability to reduce costs	+
	Financial size	+
	Efficient and effective accounting system for cost, budget and profit planning	+

(Continued)

Table 10.3   Internal Analysis (*Continued*)

	Factors	Strengths/ Weaknesses
Operations	Raw materials cost and availability	+
	Inventory control systems; inventory turnover	+
	Location of facilities; layout and utilization of facilities	−
	Economies of scale	−
	Technical efficiency of facilities and utilization of capacity	+
	Effective use of subcontracting	+
	Degree of vertical integration, value added and profit margin	NA
	Efficiency and cost/benefit of equipment	+/?
	Effective operation control procedures	+
	Cost and technological competencies relative to industry and competitors	+
	Research and development/technology/innovation	−
	Patents, trademarks and similar legal protection	−
Personnel	Management personnel	+
	Employees' skill and morale	+
	Labor relations compared to industry and competition	−
	Efficient and effective personnel policies	−
	Effective use of incentives to motivate performance	−
	Ability to level peaks and valleys of employment	+
	Employee turnover and absenteeism	+
	Specialized skills	+
	Experience	+
General Management/Organization	Organizational structure	−
	Firm's image and prestige	+
	Firm's record for achieving objectives	+
	Organization of communication system	−
	Overall organizational control system	+
	Organizational climate, culture	+
	Use of systematic procedures and techniques in decision making	−
	Top-management skill, capacities and interest	+
	Strategic planning system	+
	Intraorganizational synergy	+

Table 10.4 Comparison with the Main Competitors

	Factors	*Metal Group*	*Comp. X*	*Comp. Y*
Marketing	Firm's products/services; breadth of product line	+	+	+
	Concentration of sales in a few products or to a few customers	−	−	−
	Ability to gather needed information about markets	+	+	+
	Market share or submarket shares	+	+	+
	Product/service mix and expansion potential	+	+	+
	Channels of distribution: number, coverage and control	NA		
	Effective sales organization	+	+	+
	Product/service image, reputation and quality	+	+	+
	Imaginative, efficient and effective sales promotion and advertising	−	+	+
	Pricing strategy and pricing flexibility	+/−	+/−	+/−
	Procedures for digesting market feedback and developing new products, services or markets	−	+	+
	After-sale service and follow up	+	+	+
	Goodwill/brand loyalty	+	+	+
Finance and Accounting	Ability to raise short-term capital	+	+	+
	Ability to raise long-term capital: debt/equity	+	+	+
	Corporate-level resources	+	+	+
	Cost of capital relative to industry and competitors	−	+	+
	Tax considerations	+	+	+
	Relations with owners, investors and stockholders	+	+	+
	Leverage positions	+	+	+
	Cost of entry and barriers to entry	+	+	+
	Price-earnings ratio	+	+	+
	Working capital; flexibility of capital structure	+	+	+
	Effective cost control, ability to reduce costs	+	+	+
	Financial size	+	+	+
	Efficient and effective accounting system for cost, budget and profit planning	+	+	+

(Continued)

Table 10.4   Comparison with the Main Competitors (*Continued*)

	Factors	Metal Group	Comp. X	Comp. Y
Production/Operations/Technical	Raw materials cost and availability	+	+	+
	Inventory control systems; inventory turnover	+	?	?
	Location of facilities; layout and utilization of facilities	−	+	+
	Economies of scale	−	+	+
	Technical efficiency of facilities and utilization of capacity	+	+	+
	Effective use of subcontracting	+	?	?
	Degree of vertical integration, value added and profit margin	NA	+	+
	Efficiency and cost/benefit of equipment	+/?	+	+
	Effective operation control procedures	+	+	+
	Cost and technological competencies relative to industry and competitors	+	+	+
	Research and development/technology/innovation	−	+	+
	Patents, trademarks and similar legal protection	−	+	+
Personnel	Management personnel	+	?	?
	Employees' skill and morale	+	?	?
	Labor relations compared to industry and competition	−	−	−
	Efficient and effective personnel policies	−	+	+
	Effective use of incentives to motivate performance	−	?	?
	Ability to level peaks and valleys of employment	+	+	+
	Employee turnover and absenteeism	+	+	+
	Specialized skills	+	+	+
	Experience	+	+	+
General Management/Organization	Organizational structure	−	?	?
	Firm's image and prestige	+	+	+
	Firm's record for achieving objectives	+	+	+
	Organization of communication system	−	+	+
	Overall organizational control system	+	+	+
	Organizational climate, culture	+	?	?
	Use of systematic procedures and techniques in decision making	−	+	+
	Top-management skill, capacities and interest	+	?	?
	Strategic planning system	+	+	+
	Intraorganizational synergy	+	+	+

Table 10.5   Competitive Advantages, Success Factors, Vulnerabilities

	Factors	*Compet. Advntg*	*Success Factor*	*Vulnerability*
Marketing	Firm's products/services; breadth of product line		+	
	Concentration of sales in a few products or to a few customers			
	Ability to gather needed information about markets		+	
	Market share or submarket shares		+	
	Product/service mix and expansion potential		+	
	Channels of distribution: number, coverage and control			
	Effective sales organization		+	
	Product/service image, reputation and quality		+	
	Imaginative, efficient and effective sales promotion and advertising			+
	Pricing strategy and pricing flexibility		+/?	
	Procedures for digesting market feedback and developing new products, services or markets			+
	After-sale service and follow up		+	
	Goodwill/brand loyalty		+	
Finance and Accounting	Ability to raise short-term capital		+	
	Ability to raise long-term capital: debt/equity		+	
	Corporate-level resources		+	
	Cost of capital relative to industry and competitors			+
	Tax considerations		+	
	Relations with owners, investors and stockholders		+	
	Leverage positions		+	
	Cost of entry and barriers to entry		+	
	Price-earnings ratio		+	
	Working capital; flexibility of capital structure		+	
	Effective cost control, ability to reduce costs		+	
	Financial size		+	
	Efficient and effective accounting system for cost, budget and profit planning		+	

(Continued)

Table 10.5   Competitive Advantages, Success Factors, Vulnerabilities (*Continued*)

	Factors	Compet. Advntg	Success Factor	Vulnerability
Production/Technical	Raw materials cost and availability		+	
	Inventory control systems; inventory turnover	+?		
	Location of facilities; layout and utilization of facilities			+
	Economies of scale			+
	Technical efficiency of facilities and utilization of capacity		+	
	Effective use of subcontracting	+?		
	Degree of vertical integration, value added and profit margin			+
	Efficiency and cost/benefit of equipment		+	
	Effective operation control procedures		+	
	Cost and technological competencies relative to industry and competitors		+	
	Research and development/technology/innovation			+
	Patents, trademarks and similar legal protection			+
Personnel	Management personnel	+?		
	Employees' skill and morale	+?		
	Labor relations compared to industry and competition			
	Efficient and effective personnel policies			+
	Effective use of incentives to motivate performance			+
	Ability to level peaks and valleys of employment		+	
	Employee turnover and absenteeism		+	
	Specialized skills		+	
	Experience		+	
General Management/Organization	Organizational structure			+
	Firm's image and prestige		+	
	Firm's record for achieving objectives		+	
	Organization of communication system			+
	Overall organizational control system		+	
	Organizational climate, culture	+?		
	Use of systematic procedures and techniques in decision making			+
	Top-management skill, capacities and interest	+?		
	Strategic planning system		+	
	Intraorganizational synergy		+	

Future Design of the Organization

Opportunities for the organization (taking into account the competitive advantages of the enterprise and matching them with potential positive scenarios of the sector), and therefore the strategic objective, main goals and main strategies to be achieved over the next five years were indicated through brainstorming and group works.

Organization Opportunity Definition

Continuing to grow in NAMET and Europe by using the benefits of economies of scale factor (thus increasing efficiency and reducing costs) and focusing on a similar product portfolio.

Strategic Objective

Being a preferred supplier by the multinational and potential customers.

Main Goals

Table 10.6 shows the main goals. In this study, internal factors such as workforce, technology, organization and management, operational issues, products and market positions, financial characteristics, etc. were taken into consideration.

Table 10.6   Main Goals

	Goals	Definition
Financial & Market	Target markets	Europe, NAMET, Russia, International companies
	Product range	Personal Care, Pharmaceutical, Food, Stationery, Cosmetics
	Sales volume and profitability for the planned period	Turnover of 60 million € at the end of 2018, EBITDA 20%
	Comparative growth expectations	35% revenue growth at the end of the fifth year
	Countries to operate in	Turkey, Bulgaria, Russia, Dubai - Iran, France, Germany
	Regional concentration	Turkey, Balkans, United Kingdom, Central European Countries, Russia, Middle East, Egypt, Tunisia, Algeria, Central and North America
	Strategic partnerships considered	No

(Continued)

Table 10.6   Main Goals (*Continued*)

	Goals	Definition
Operations-/Personnel/Management	Organization	Review and create the organizational structure according to the five-year revised targets.
		Creation and implementation of a backup and development organization for key positions.
	Training and experience	For the need for additional blue-collar personnel, employees with sufficient competencies are recruited from today and subjected to continuous training together with existing employees.
		Complete general trainings for the white collar which will strengthen their corporate culture, then plan managerial trainings for person-based needs.
	Wage and compensation	Enable high-performing employees receiving premiums.
	Investment goals	On the packaging side, the existing 11 lines will be increased to 13 lines in total by adding 2 new lines. One of the new lines will be installed in Bulgaria.
		One of the 6 lines in the laminate is being renewed.
		For aerosol, the purchase of a new line is planned. A new rental place is also considered for production.
	Labor turnover rate	%2
	Safety regulations	Work in strict accordance with the rules of OHS and related legislation.
	Environmental standards	To be fully compliant with both environmental legislation and the high standards expectations of our customers and to be shown as an exemplary packaging manufacturer.
	Technology and equipment choice	Replacing four of the six laminated machines with new machines within five years.
		The new Aerosol line will also be able to produce bottles.
	Scrap rates	Aerosol: <4.0%
		Lamine: <2.9%
		Aluminum: <7.5%
	Maintenance and repair policies	Installing and operationalizing the TPM system
	Long-term capacity plans	Aluminum: 450*1.2 million
		Laminated: 140*1.2 million
		Aerosol: 160*1.2 million
	Labor level	The goal will be set.
	Production quantities	Aluminum: 450 million
		Laminated: 140 million
		Aerosol: 160 million
	Inventory level	The goal will be set.

Main Strategies

In the light of the opportunities and main goals identified above, and according to the "components of strategy" (Ansoff 1970), it seems appropriate that the preference of the enterprise in the product-market position should be to develop new nearby markets with existing products. Therefore, *market development* is one of the main strategies.

Market development:

- After the research, creating an external structure to monitor proactive sales activities in Russia – Dubai (including Iran) on behalf of metal packaging. This strategy may include office and/or team building with a focus on Europe and the UK.
- Creating synergies with the plastics companies in the Group.
- Increasing company awareness.
- Carrying out promotional activities professionally (participation in fairs, web, etc.).

Referring to the "general competitive strategies" (Porter 1998), the most basic competitive advantage of this enterprise is its low cost and a narrower scope rather than global as a field of activity that seems appropriate. So, *cost focusing* is another of its main strategies.

Cost focusing:

- Operational excellence.
- Reducing waste with improvements to be made and reducing unit costs with efficiency-increasing effects.
- Economies of scale (increasing capacity and renewing technology).
- Making the TPM system operational.
- OEE upgrade.
- Keeping personnel costs under control.
- Improving inventory turnover rates and aging.
- Synergy in purchasing.
- Carrying out energy procurement in a way to cover all subcontractor enterprises.
- Examining investment incentives and grants in Bulgaria and Turkey.
- Finding the most suitable financing for investments.

- Review and create the organizational structure according to the five-year revised goals.
- Complete general trainings that will strengthen the corporate culture of the white collar, then plan their personal training needs.
- Finding an alternative location and preparing an ideal facility plan.
- Approaching green factory and energy-saving concepts for the new investment.
- Reviewing all processes all over and designing more productive systems by taking process management training and consultancy services.
- Establish a backup and development system for key positions.
- Recruit employees with sufficient competencies for additional blue-collar personnel needs and subject them to continuous training and certification together with existing employees.
- Establish a system for high-performance employees receiving premiums.
- Planning the lean layout and material handling systems for the existing factory and warehouse facilities.

Chapter 11

Information Bureaus

As an Information Bureau, the institution continues its activities to meet all kinds of information requests in economic, social and cultural fields within the framework of relations with the European Union and to serve as a reliable reference point. Due to its only competent position in the field of activity as a public institution and its founding mission, there was a need for the institution to continue to work through internal analysis.

Therefore, the strategic planning study has been developed through the analysis of internal factors of the organization. In order to determine the evolution of the organization from past to present and the strengths and weaknesses they have created in the business structure, the following results have been obtained through brainstorming and group studies. In this study, internal factors such as workforce, technology, organization and management, operational issues, products and market positions, financial characteristics, etc. are taken into consideration.

Evolution of the Organization

1996   The first Information Bureau was established.
Promotional activities.
Target audience activities – meetings.
Customs Union meetings and visits.
Second Information Bureau was established.
Visit to Brussels in the name of institutionalization.
Protocol was signed between the Chamber of Commerce and the Delegation.

DOI: 10.4324/9781003519614-13

Coordinators were designated by the Chambers.

Computer communication with Brussels has begun.

The training of delegation coordinators began.

Third Information Bureau was established and support negotiations began.

1997 Other Information Bureaus were established.

Coordination meetings have begun.

Logo usage has been started.

The Luxembourg summit affected relations.

Some sample events were organized.

2002 The network definition was introduced.

An e-mail group has been established.

2003 ESİAD performed a service for Information Bureaus.

2004 Budget contracts started to be made on an annual basis.

The budget has been increased.

Promotional materials were prepared.

Events for local needs have begun.

2005 The logo definition has changed.

Inspection visits to the member states have begun.

Representatives of NGOs and the media were sent to Brussels.

Cultural activities began.

Some sample events were organized.

2006 A consortium of four institutions was established.

Some sample events were organized.

2007 Goodwill agreements with Chambers of Commerce and other bureaus have been made.

Some sample events were organized.

Current Status of the Organization

- There is a need for specialization.
- Competence in organizing events has been achieved.
- Good relations with the press developed.
- There is competence in the use of budget.
- Prestige began to be achieved.

- Inter-institutional communication has been improved.
- The reporting system has begun to settle down.
- There is no shortage of technological infrastructure.
- There are problems with time management.
- There is a multi-headedness in the administration.
- Although there is budgetary independence with the Chamber, there is dependence on organizing events.
- There is a disconnection between the Chamber management and the Delegation's purpose and target group.
- It is difficult to find promotional tools.
- The target group does not know where their location is.
- There are deficiencies in the ability to localize information.
- Communication with the headquarter is not functioning well enough and is incomplete.
- Currently demands from the headquarter can be met, but there may be more additional demand coming.
- The expectations of the bureaus are not asked.
- Having the information of knowing which publication is coming in advance can make events more rationally organized.
- Relations with public institutions are strong. However, in practice, problematic relationships can happen at any time due to the personnel issues.
- Ability and diversity to deploy services is good.
- Target audience come to the bureau if they need it.
- Not every region of Turkey can be reached.

Strengths

- Ability to use local resources.
- Ability to organize and deploy services.
- Strong relationships with the institutions and local media.
- Ability to reach various target groups.
- To be the reference point in the province.

Weaknesses

- Lack of communication between information providers.
- Identification of needs and use of the right tools for them.
- Lack of sharing among coordinators.

- The fact that the job descriptions are influenced by the host institutions (for example Chambers) (it can be said that there is no autonomy).
- Lack of manpower.
- Lack of goals and strategies.
- Experiencing weaknesses in the continuity of activities.
- Lack of protection from external factors.

Success Factors

- The necessity of budget optimization and plan.
- Qualified manpower.
- The need to determine general strategies and objectives.
- National recognition.
- To be able to develop innovative approaches.
- Determination of job descriptions.
- Creation of network awareness – systematic flow of information.
- Realization of qualified trainings.

Future Design of the Organization

In the light of the results obtained in the above studies, the strategic objective, main goals and main strategies to be achieved for the next five years for the organization are indicated by the brainstorming and group work.

Strategic Objective

As a reliable and impartial source of information, to be an area of interest for target groups by informing and raising awareness of Turkey.

Main Goals

Information Network:

- All of Turkey

Target:

- Primary and secondary school students
- University students
- Local targets

Goals for Services:

■ To organize activities in accordance with its internal dynamism in each region and to ensure participation in joint activities through the central coordination unit.
■ To make a national event permanent.
■ To organize activities together with the Ministry of National Education and/or universities.

Promotional Goals:

■ National and regional awareness.
■ Using the national media.
■ Producing visual material.
■ Preparing periodicals.
■ Visit the relevant units.

Financial Goals:

■ Sponsors
■ Target group contribution to local events.
■ Increasing the budget and distributing it according to certain criteria.

Organizational Goals:

■ Re-defining job descriptions and agreeing with strategic partners.
■ Increasing the qualified workforce, improving the working environment and systems.
■ Strengthening intra-network communication.
■ Increasing motivation.

Technology Goals:

■ Creation of an intranet.
■ Public web site
■ Webcam
■ Obtaining service consultancy.

Main Strategies

In the light of the main goals set out above and according to the "components of the strategy" (Ansoff 1970), it seems appropriate that the organization's preference in the position of the service-information network is to develop the entire Turkish information network with existing services. Therefore, *improving the information network* is its main strategy.

Improving the information network:

- Sponsors
- Public institutions and organizations
- Attracting local authorities
- Media
- NGO
- Universities and educational institutions
- Development through strategic collaborations such as host organizations and Delegation.

Chapter 12

Plastic Packaging Co.

The company, which produces plastic products with injection technology, was established in 1990 with the aim of producing plastic cap and accessories and adding an innovative perspective to the sector. As a world brand without sacrificing quality standards, the company has been continuing to invest in innovation.

Trends Affecting the Sector

In the brainstorming sessions, the following results were obtained by reviewing the trends of external factors such as demographic, economic, legal-political, technological and social changes, market dynamics, customer expectations, competitive conditions, strategies and objectives of competitors, suppliers, substitutes on the plastic product production sector over the next five years:

- The plastics industry is developing.
- The need to reduce cost without deteriorating quality.
- The advantage of recycling.
- It is better for consumer health than metal and glass.
- The export advantage of being small in volume.
- Plastic products are cheap.
- It has a technology that is easy to operate.
- The importance of in-house production.
- Recognition of production technology.

DOI: 10.4324/9781003519614-14

- Decline of small firms.
- Having a chance to create a niche market for small companies.
- Production of materials of various colors.
- Laser printing process, IML (in-mold labeling) advantage.
- The importance of high service quality.
- It is not necessary to be a mold maker.
- Ability to win new customers by reducing costs in injection technology.
- Portable and easy to use.
- Increase in the use and consumption of plastic in the world by 10% and machine manufacturing by 5%.
- The shift of plastics manufacturing to the east of Europe.
- Ability to produce low quantities with rapid prototype molds.
- Increasing population and demand.
- The necessity of having a wide range of products and a high production efficiency.
- Under-the-stairs production and unfair competition are a negative factor in pricing.
- Environmental pollution caused by plastic.
- China's growing competitiveness.
- The creativity factor is very important in the sector.
- Specialization in the lower layers of the sector becomes evident.
- Increase in the cost of mold if the production quantities are not high.
- Harm of plastic to human health.
- The multiplicity of competing companies on the basis of producers.
- The lack of vocational schools in Turkey, the scarcity of trained staff and especially the lack of quality injection molders.
- Global-sourcing.
- Orientation towards large-scale suppliers.
- Low demand in Turkey.
- Long design time of new products.
- The negative impact of seasonal conditions on quality.
- Lack of customer loyalty.
- Increase of the main raw material producer monopoly.
- The public turns a blind eye to unfair competition in some cases.
- The establishment of production centers in Poland and Hungary, but they have quality problems.
- European countries that are outsourcing turn inward due to unemployment.

- The growing importance of economies of scale and specialization.
- Lack of trade agreements for some countries.
- Distribution and shipping problems due to delivery points.
- The threat of compression technology to the cap.
- Due to the low initial capital, other manufacturers can easily enter the market.
- The importance of branding.
- The necessity of allocating high funds for quality products.
- Rotational mold threats of international producers.
- The fact that competitors have their own mold workshops.
- There are mold making injection companies in Turkey.
- Increasing the need for both standardization and customer-oriented production.
- Lack of quality injection mold maker in Turkey.

Positive/Negative Scenarios

The potential positive and negative scenarios for the plastic product production sector over the next five years are set out in the following definitions, as a result of group works, taking into account the significant developments in the sector worldwide and nationwide mentioned above.

Positive Scenarios

- The fact that the plastics market is developing and growing.
- Innovation-oriented development of the sector.
- The obligation to be the solution partner of the customer.
- To be able to create regional market opportunities with the ability to standardize.

Negative Scenarios

- Increased competitiveness of Chinese manufacturers.
- Turkey's technological inadequacy in the sector continues.
- Global sourcing.
- Rapid change of customer expectations.
- The barrier to entry of new players into the sector is low.
- Export policies are not yielding sufficient results.

Evolution of the Organization

1962   First cap production.
Two "Bottom-felt" machines.

1976   Sixteen plastic injection machines.

1977   Separate molds were started to be produced for each type of cap (up to 48 cavities.)

1979   High cavity caps began to be produced.
Number of machines reduced to 3 (equal capacity to 16 machines)
The machines were sold, the surplus was gathered under the roof of another company.
Moving to the new place.
Five additional machines were added.
There was the participation of new large companies in the customer portfolio.

1983   Gen. Dir. was appointed.
Sixteen machines.
Newly joined customer caps (molds with 48–72 cavities.)
4–8 cavity molds for some customers.
Number of employees 21.

1984   Moved to a bigger place.
The "insert" mold is activated.

1986   The first domestic "Batesfelt" machine (4 small, 1 large.)
The old ones began to be sold.
For the big customer, liquid vim, lux and shampoo caps came into play.

1987   It was decided not to buy machines from domestic machine manufacturers.
Agreement with the Oil-Labor Union.

1988   Seven "Makplast" machines were purchased.
Other machines began to be sold.

1989   Strike.
There are seventeen injection machines.
The use of "master batch" was introduced.

1990   Injection molding machines are under the roof of Plasal.
        Production for the main customer with 7–8 machines.
        "Hot-runner" molds were introduced.

1991   New Gen. Dir.
        Moved to the current new location.
        Outsourcing manufacturing of raw materials.
        Three "Ferromatic" injection machines.

1994   All injection molding machines were collected at the same location.
        Transition to modern molding technique.
        A total of 20 elements and 12 machines.
        There was the first pause in the performance that has risen so far.

1997   Seventeen "Ferromatic" machines.
        A total of 36 employees.
        New responsibilities in the organization (e.g., additional,
        manufacturing, quality assurance.)

1998   Closed loop cooling system was installed.

1999   ISO-9001 was obtained.
        Transition to active sales activity.

2001   The company began to be known by name.
        Exit from contract manufacturing.
        A total of 24 elements and 20 machines.

2003   New injection molding machines (17 units) joined the machine park.
        A total of 36 elements and 35 machines.

Current Status of the Organization

Considering the stages of the enterprise from past to present, the following results were obtained through brainstorming and group studies in order to determine the strengths and weaknesses they have created in the business structure. In this study, internal factors such as workforce, technology, organization and management, operational issues, products and market positions, financial characteristics, etc. are taken into consideration.

■ The possibility of experiencing location problems.
■ A predisposition to technology has developed.

- High cavity molds are needed.
- We are not flexible and ready for new customers.
- Dependence on some large corporations.
- The company corporate ID is not ready.
- It depends on the conditions of the country.
- Marketing skills are poor – there are no staff.
- Costs are low.
- No exports.
- Insufficient level of development in manpower.
- Sufficient level of technology.
- The weakness of the modern information technology infrastructure.
- There is no R&D work and innovation is weak.
- The financial infrastructure and credibility are good.
- Our testimonials and understanding of quality are good.
- A predominantly manufacturing-oriented approach prevails.
- Even if there is technology, there are no qualified operators.
- Workforce flexibility even under challenging conditions.

Strengths

- Strong and good references.
- Workforce with high motivation, commitment to the organization and experience.
- Technological infrastructure has caught up with the age in operational terms.
- Being open to innovations.
- Strong financing structure.
- Competence in product quality.

Weaknesses

- Inability to innovate.
- Organizational deficiency.
- Dependence on some main customers.
- Location and in-plant layout problems.
- Inability to be customer-centric.
- Lack of mold portfolio.
- Lack of a management operating system.
- Marketing – the inadequacy of sales strategy and function.

Future Design of the Organization

In the light of the results obtained in the above studies, the strategic objective, main goals and main strategies to be achieved for the organization for the next five years are indicated by the brainstorming and group work.

Strategic Objective

To be the solution partner for the expectations of all customers who use and can use plastic cap and complementary packaging components produced with injection technology with innovations and creativity that create added value and with its expert staff who use technologies suitable for the age.

Main Goals

Market Goals:

- Export to all over the world.
- Regions with existing customer portfolio in the country.
- Product range (standard and featured)
- 50% export.

Financial Goals:

It was deemed appropriate to determine it with a detailed study.

Investment Goals:

Skilled staff/following the developments in the world.
Application Center (Teknopark)

↓

Rapid Prototyping Processes

Organization Goals:

- Marketing – together with group companies.
- Overseas – dealership
- Sales (domestic and export)
- R&D

■ IT
■ Non-cumbersome, participatory and inquisitive, able to perform horizontal and vertical managerial work with synergistic coordination.

Main Strategies

In the light of the main goals set out above, and according to the "components of strategy" approach (Ansoff 1970), it seems appropriate that the preference of the enterprise in the product-market position should be to develop new nearby markets with more innovative new products. Hence, *diversification* is the main strategy.

Diversification:

■ To be open to new market opportunities.
■ Strategic partnerships or collaborations with experience in the fields of training, innovation and formwork.
■ To cooperate with group companies in innovation issues and also to evaluate their customer potential.

Chapter 13

Port Management

Company which is founded by a group of entrepreneurs consisting of land and sea managers and employees who have worked in the field of maritime transportation for many years, has the title of the school of the Turkish maritime sector. In the port facility, the company provides port loading and unloading services and warehouse management, etc. services.

Environmental Analysis

The effects of external factors such as demographic, economic, legal-political, technological and social changes, market dynamics, customer expectations, competitive conditions, strategies and objectives of competitors, etc. on the transportation and port management sector for the next five years were reviewed in brainstorming and group study sessions and the following results were obtained:

Macroeconomic Analysis

Macroeconomic variables affect enterprises and the industries in which they are functioning and are not under the control of the enterprises. Macroeconomic variables are as follows:

- Demographical
- Economical

DOI: 10.4324/9781003519614-15

- Legal-Political
- Technological
- Social-Cultural

This analysis should be carried out first in relation to the global and then to the region and the country. The aim is to find out the effects of macroeconomic variables on the sector, from the perspectives of different stakeholders.

The effects of macroeconomic variables on the transportation and port management sector over the next five years were reviewed in brainstorming and group study sessions and the following results were obtained:

- The increase in competition in parallel with the increasing liberalization of trade in the world, the prolongation of transportation distances with the weight of global and regional organizations have brought the speed element to the forefront. This situation has increased the importance of delivering raw materials and processed products to buyers at low cost and on time and has expanded the use of combined transportation systems supported by logistics services.
- The general principle in EU transport policies is to strike a balance between economic development and society's demands for quality and safety in order to create a modern, sustainable transportation system. It is proposed to find alternatives to road transportation such as short sea transportation, rail system and inland waterways.
- In EU transportation policy, transportation infrastructure is based on public financing for regional, national or union purposes. In addition to national funds, the budget allocated for the EU's structural funds, cohesion funds and Trans-European networks is used to finance the transportation policy action program. Union funds are mostly linked to the provision of infrastructure connections, multi-functionality and contribution to the development of more security conditions.
- EU transport legislation aims to improve the functioning of the internal market by supporting safe, efficient, environmentally sound and user-friendly transport services.
- The volume of international maritime has been on the upward trend for a long time.
- In parallel with the development in world trade volume, strong increases are also seen in container trade volume.

- In the dry bulk cargo sector, China has become the most influential player in the steel industry and has become more influential in the increase in trade volume than it has done in previous years.
- The increase in world trade volume is progressing. The world maritime trade volume consists of the transportation of highly valuable trade goods by the bulk method.
- Normally, growth in industrial production is a better indicator of transportation demand.
- It is expected that the world's shipping market rise will continue.
- Fluctuations in many segments of the market, particularly in the dry bulk and container ship categories, will largely depend on developments in China.
- The United States will continue to be the largest oil importer country for many years to come.
- Turkish exports have been one of the basic elements of the country's macroeconomic development. Due to its high share in the general export of industrial products, the export growth rate of these products has been influential in the overall export increase.
- It is seen that Turkey's imports are also increasing continuously. The increase in imports was influenced by economic growth, the increase in manufacturing industry production, exchange rate developments and increases in commodity prices, especially oil. Within this framework, imports of intermediate and capital goods, which are linked to production and export, are also constantly increasing.
- Turkey is taking the necessary steps for full membership to the EU. Although it has not yet happened, this will bring a new dimension to the integration of the country's transportation system into the international combined network.
- The delays in the replacement of the war and conflict in the Middle East by the peace process also make it necessary for the trade routes of the Middle Eastern countries to pass through Turkey.
- Functionally, another area that expects service from Turkey's ports is the energy sector. In the long run, coal comes to the fore in energy needs.
- Turkey will have to meet its energy needs with coal-based thermal power plants in the coming years. The coal to be imported is transported by large tonnage ships from overseas countries such as Australia, North America, South Africa.
- On the other hand, the Russian Federation and Kazakhstan are among the important coal-exporting countries.

■ The most important infrastructure requirement for coal to be transported by sea is port facilities. With the current capacities of today's ports in Turkey, partial of the demand can be met. New ports are needed for the remaining needs.

■ In the past period, great innovations and changes in the technological field of port management have established themselves and have become an important factor that forces the unity between countries. Since the 1960s, the system has been changed in order to ensure speed, safety and regularity in maritime transportation in the world.

■ As a result of the transformation of the transportation chain from region to region to include all modes of transportation, the concept of a monopolistic hinterland in ports no longer existed.

■ All countries agree that a single port point, road, railway line or waterway no longer makes sense, but becomes important when planned together.

■ In container transportation, ports are categorized as main or feeder ports. The containers that reach the main ports by the main transit lines are transferred to smaller tonnage ships and sent to smaller ports, which we call feeder ports. From here it enters the network of rail, road or waterway, reaching its destination.

■ Long-distance container transportation between the Far East and European countries passes through the Eastern Mediterranean, the Suez Canal, the Red Sea and today it is served by the ports of Malta, Piraeus, Limassol, Alexandria as the main ports.

■ In Turkey, where 90% of its foreign trade is carried out by sea, and from the ports and piers of the country, which has an important place in the transit transportation from the industrialized countries of Europe to the Middle East countries, mixed goods including bulk liquids, bulk solids, containers, industrial products, agricultural products, timber and other cargoes were handled.

■ While the container and combined transportation system is applied in the most efficient way in the world, as a result of the fact that the ports of Turkey are planned, built and operated in a conventional way, these ports provide only feeder service.

■ This situation, which has clearly developed in favor of the highway in Turkey as well as in the European Union in domestic transportation, is shifting toward the sea route in foreign trade. In terms of both the quantity and the value of the cargo transported in Turkey's foreign trade, maritime transportation has the lion's share.

- In Turkey, the international road transportation fleet has reached to the saturation point in terms of its capacity. This situation suggests the necessity of increasing the number of the road fleet.
- However, both the competition brought by the Eastern European countries that have just joined the EU and the EU's policies to reduce road transport and the restrictions on transit increase the estimates that capacity utilization may decline.
- The predominant share of international goods transportation by road is in shipments to Europe. Next, it is Russia and the CIS countries, as well as the countries of the Middle East.
- Ports in Turkey have a cargo handling capacity of approximately 120 million tons/year and the total berthing length of the ship exceeds 33 km. In addition, there are oil and petroleum products loading and unloading facilities with a capacity of approximately 160–170 million tons/year.
- The year 2005 can be considered as the beginning year of transformation for Turkey's ports. The privatization process of six ports operated by TCDD, which are among the most important ports in Turkey, was initiated in the second half of 2005. In the first stage, the privatization process of Mersin and İskenderun ports had already started.
- On the other hand, the ports built and operated by the private sector in Turkey have increased their performance day by day.

Industry Competitiveness and Development

What most influences a business are the groups that make up the competition within the industry in which it operates (e.g., firms in the industry, potential start-ups and markets and customers, etc.). The effects of these forces determine the intensity of competition in an industry.

The effects of industry development and competition on the transportation and port management sector over the next five years were reviewed in brainstorming and group study sessions and the following conclusions were obtained:

- The market consists of the ancillary services required for the retribution, handling, storage and transportation of all kinds of solid, liquid, gas commercial commodities brought by sea to the ports and the transportation to the hinterlands by combined transportation and the fulfillment of these services.

■ The customer attaches great importance to servicing factors such as reliability, shortening transit times, speed, increasing the undamaged delivery rate, keeping sufficient stock, meeting orders quickly, performing distribution quickly, security and accuracy.

■ On the basis of tons, regional sea loading constitutes 17.33% and unloading 24.91% of Turkey.

■ Due to the BTC pipeline, the importance of the region has increased.

■ With the full completion of the GAP project in Turkey, the need for transportation will increase as needed by the industries to be established here.

■ Container transportation is increasing day by day and today 25% of the world's container traffic uses Mediterranean traffic.

■ The reconstruction of post-war Iraq will revitalize the region economically. In this new period, as a result of trade liberalization and economic revival in Iraq, there will be an increase in Turkey's exports to Iraq with the advantage of proximity to the region.

■ Turkey's exports to Middle Eastern countries have increased over the years and there will be an increase in transit freight transportation depending on the conditions.

■ The main container transportation lines pass through the Eastern Mediterranean. This further increases the importance of Mersin and İskenderun ports.

■ If the ports of Iskenderun and Mersin serve as the main ports, Turkey will be able to create an indispensable corridor in transit traffic.

■ In terms of their location in the Eastern Mediterranean, especially the ports of Mersin and Izmir are growing steadily in terms of transshipment.

■ Of these, the ports of Mersin and Iskenderun have played a significant active role in terms of transit traffic, especially for Iran, Iraq and Middle Eastern countries.

■ Due to the geographical location of this region, it is important to emphasize the use of Ro-Ro ramps for military purposes in the light of the practices of previous years.

■ Combined transport affects the hinterland of the port with road and rail connections. Export shipments to Middle Eastern countries by road have an important share. The main destination for these transports is Iraq.

- In the ports of the southern region of Turkey, there are no services to meet the needs of breakdown repairs, periodic maintenance and docking of ships.
- In the Eastern Mediterranean, there is an increasingly intense competition between ports in order to get a share of the transit cargo. In this race, Turkey's ports have the chance due to their positions in the Mediterranean.
- On the other hand, with the completion of the GAP project, the need to review the port capacities in parallel with the needs of the industries here has emerged. Accordingly, there are Iskenderun and Mersin ports for the entrances and exits of the industrial needs that will develop in the region.

Positive/Negative Scenarios

The potential positive and negative scenarios for the transportation and port management sector over the next five years are set out in the following definitions, as a result of group work, taking into account the above-mentioned worldwide and nationwide significant developments in the sector.

Positive Scenarios

- Due to Turkey's geographical location, with the view that the crisis in the Middle East Region will continue, it is obvious that Mersin and the Gulf of Iskenderun in particular will be a very serious transit route. In addition, the fact that the shipments to the Mediterranean region are in an increasing trend and that 90% of Turkey's foreign trade is carried out by sea increases the attractiveness of Mersin and İskenderun Gulf.
- The fact that the GAP project will be completed and as a result of the serious industrialization that will occur here, it will allow the increase of trade in the region and thus the intensification of port activities in the Mersin and İskenderun Gulf.
- The existence of opportunities that will ensure that the operating conditions of Mersin and the Gulf of Iskenderun, which will become a transit center for the transportation of fuel, natural gas and oil-derived products to Europe through Russia and the Caucasus, will be maximized.
- With the foresight that the political stability in Turkey will continue for a certain period of time and that there will be no significant changes in

the legal order within the first five years, investments can be carried out without interruption.

- Positive impact of the good relations with Turkic states.
- Especially in Turkey, there is no facility to allow the handling of post-panamax vessels.
- Facilities that enable the rapid handling of the materials in the container with safety management systems are not yet available in Turkey.

Negative Scenarios

- Terrorist incidents have been increasing recently.
- The escalation of political tension in the Middle East and the decline of commercial activities in that region due to the anticipated blockades and embargoes.
- Developments that may occur if a possible coalition that may arise at the end of the election adversely affect political stability (cancellation of tenders, failure to grant the desired permits, bureaucratic difficulties, etc.)
- The negative effects of an economic crisis on the exchange rate and inflation.
- If introduced, the new taxes will have a negative impact on investment and operating costs.
- Negative effects of the Kyoto Protocol, which affects environmental factors, on the cost of the industry.
- Abolition of agricultural subsidies.
- The fact that the owners of big capital are in conflict with nation-states.

Current Status of the Organization

Considering the stages of the enterprise from past to present, the following results were obtained through brainstorming and group studies in order to determine the strengths and weaknesses that they have created in the business structure. In this study, internal factors such as workforce, technology, organization and management, operational issues, products and market positions, financial characteristics, etc. are taken into consideration.

■ A group of entrepreneurs, consisting of senior managers and employees with sea and land-related logistics experience, who have worked for many years have established the organization with the aim of continuing the maritime transportation mission.

■ The organization, which has an ISO 9001-2000 quality certificate in Ship and Port Facilities Security and Training, is authorized as a recognized security organization (RSO) on behalf of the Turkish state within the scope of the Ship and Port Security Code (ISPS Code). Within the scope of ISPS, it successfully continues its services of inspecting ships and issuing International Ship Security Certificates.

Strengths

■ The founders' vast business experience and achievements in maritime and port management dating back to the past.

■ Recognition by a very wide base in the maritime industry.

■ The sense of perseverance and trust that its founders and employees have in the national and international maritime sector.

■ The advantages of having a corporate structure with ISO 9001:2000 quality certificate.

■ The customer portfolio is wide enough and the necessary agency network can be easily established.

■ Due to the accumulated knowledge and experience in both port and maritime management, a significant contribution can be made to the development of new services and the improvement of existing ones with respect to competitors.

■ Adaptability to developing technology.

■ Availability of the possibility of providing different types of transportation and other services to third parties.

■ Availability of a railway connection within the plant.

■ The presence of pipe connection lines that provide the possibility of loading and unloading fuel oil and liquid products.

■ The lack of units in the southern region for providing repair services to ships and the possibility of providing this service to the clients.

Weaknesses

- The lack of possibility of new construction due to the fact that the existing facility is within the coastal edge line and the bureaucratic difficulties that may arise in ensuring the continuation of the permits obtained.
- Insufficient level of company capital structure.
- The existing plant has outdated technology.
- The pier does not fully respond to the work that is planned to be done.
- The professional staff of human resources has not yet been formed.
- Fuel and dry cargo handling are carried out at the same pier.

Competitive Advantages, Success Factors, Key Vulnerabilities

Additionally, the firm's strengths and weaknesses were compared with the main competitors (described in the following pages) to find out the firm's competitive advantages, success factors and weaknesses. In short, we can say the following:

- Competitive advantages – factors that give the business an advantage over its competitors and key factors on which the strategy of the business will be formed.
- Success factors – important factors that the business must have but are also typically found in every profitable competitor. It does not constitute a potential source for any strategic advantage.
- Key vulnerabilities – factors in which the business does not currently have the necessary skills, knowledge or resources to compete effectively.

Rivalry

Pier X

It has been opened to service only for the purchase of raw materials and the export of finished products. Later, general port services started to be provided and all kinds of cargo except passenger, container and bulk liquid cargoes were loaded and discharged.

Depending on the tonnage of the ships, 4–6 ships can dock at the pier. The annual cargo handling capacity is 1,800,000 tons, there is an open storage area and there is no closed storage area.

As a result of their establishment purposes, they serve the needs of their companies and serve third parties with a very small capacity.

Its services provide uninterrupted service in the types of goods such as coal, mine, fertilizer, all kinds of bulk and bagged cargo, logs, iron, logs, timber, citrus fruits and work with maximum supply.

Pier Y

It is engaged in general port activities for all types of cargo except passenger, container and bulk liquid cargoes.

Depending on the tonnage of the ships, 5–8 ships can dock at the pier. The annual cargo handling capacity is 3.500.000 tons and there is an open and closed storage area. The bonded warehouse is a closed area and customs open area and works with maximum supply.

As a result of their establishment purposes, they usually serve the needs of their companies and serve third parties with a very small capacity.

Port Z

The port, which is open to freight and passenger traffic and whose infrastructure has been realized with large investments, has been adversely affected after the Gulf crisis in 1990 and is operating with its waste capacity.

Pilotage and towing services of the ships arriving and departing from the port are provided by the sea vehicles and units established within its own structure.

There are a total of nine docks in the said port. Cargo handling capacity is 3.500.000 tons/year.

Competitive Advantages

- The founders' vast business experience and achievements in maritime and port management dating back to the past.
- Recognition by a very wide base in the maritime industry.
- The sense of perseverance and trust that its founders and employees have in the national and international maritime sector.
- The existing facility has been granted a landfill permit.
- The fact that there are no units in the southern region to provide repair services to ships and that this service can be provided by the company.

■ The port area is within the largest freight traffic in the Mediterranean Region and they have the only operation in this region where the railway connection comes all the way to the facility.

■ Availability of a conveyor belt system that transports bulk products to warehouses.

■ These two different methods of discharge differentiate the facility from other piers and ports.

■ There is an open and closed storage area above the pier area and there are steel tanks with floating roofs and pipes connected to the pier with an exproof installation feature to store all kinds of liquid products.

■ Having a pipeline and pumping station connected to the pier for the products to be taken to the warehouses.

■ Having truck loading stations for loading products stored in tanks.

■ The existing pier has the possibility of berthing large tonnage ships.

■ To have open and closed tanks made of steel for the storage of all kinds of liquid products and to have the necessary arrangements for the storage and loading of liquid products to land tankers with the existing pipelines at the pier.

■ The availability of free space on the backside of the plant.

Success Factor

■ Keeping customer satisfaction at the highest level, equipping facilities and equipment with the most modern technology and ensuring maximum profitability with economical, rentable and most appropriate conditions that keep up with the era.

Key Vulnerabilities

■ Provision of similar services in the surrounding ports and creation of competition.

■ Failure to obtain permission to use liquid cargo storage facilities.

■ Technologically all of the competitors are in a better position and they have a certain customer portfolio.

■ Port Z, which is in the process of being privatized, is the most serious competitor that can be financially strong after the new owners take over the operation.

Future Design of the Organization

Opportunities for the organization (taking into account the competitive advantages of the enterprise and matching them with potential positive scenarios of the sector), and therefore the strategic objective, main goals and main strategies to be achieved over the next five years are indicated by the brainstorming and group work sessions.

Organization's Opportunity Definition

- To get a share from the increasing sea transportation due to the regional feature.
- Since 25% of container transportation uses the Mediterranean route, to get a share from this transportation.
- Due to the lack of a technical repair unit in the region, to provide services to ships in this regard.
- To carry out Ro-Ro and train transportation, by means of Ro-Ro and train ferry ramps.
- Store petroleum products and liquid cargo.
- Storing chemical cargo.
- To provide transportation and storage services within the scope of combined transportation.
- To be a flexi-tank service provider.

Main Goals

Organization and Operational Goals:

- It is aimed that the people within the existing organization are experts in port management, warehousing, transportation and technical issues.
- Starting work on the modernization of the facility and the possibility of servicing post-panamax vessels with technological innovations.
- Making the necessary infrastructure preparations for container transportation.
- Achieving a capacity utilization rate of 100% in port services in increments of 20% each year.
- In line with the rehabilitation of the facility, the construction of a ramp of Ro-Ro and train ferry.

- Obtaining the necessary usage licenses and permits for the use of fuel tanks to third parties.
- Improvement of maintenance workshops, provision of ship maintenance and repair and docking technical services.
- Making dry and liquid cargo tanks available to third parties.
- Construction of container breaks and introduction of safety management systems that inspect containers with X-ray and gamma-ray rays.
- Depending on the expectations of the customer in the services to be provided, to make maximum use of the technological infrastructure and the developments in strong information systems in order to realize the services quickly and correctly.

Marketing Goals:

- A 20% share in port services in the first year.
- Leasing of existing warehouses.
- Gaining additional income by providing the technical service capabilities of the existing maintenance workshops.
- Creating an important logistics terminal in the region in terms of transportation, storage and technical services.
- By turning to container transportation and accordingly being among the first two facilities in the region.
- Creating the above-mentioned services from ancillary service derivatives such as warehousing, transportation, etc. to shipowners and agencies. In addition to these, firms of iron and steel, coal, cement, agricultural sectors are also targeted.

Main Strategies

In the light of the opportunities and main goals identified above, and according to the "components of strategy" (Ansoff 1970), it seems appropriate that the preference of the enterprise in the product-market position should be to develop new nearby markets with existing and new services. Therefore, *diversification* is one of the main strategies.

According to "general competitive strategies" (Porter 1998), differentiation seems to be the most basic competitive advantage that this enterprise can have, and a narrower scope rather than global as a field of activity seems appropriate. So, *differentiation focusing* is another one of its main strategies.

Diversification and differentiation focusing:

- In the realization of these goals, cooperation will be made with companies with international and national experiences and power.
- The broad recognition of the company's founders within the maritime industry and their good working relationships with this environment will be able to help its services achieving greater success.
- Being a solution partner of customers who open up to the outside world, especially with its wide infrastructure and abilities in international maritime and land transportation.
- Not only handling of the cargoes of the customers but also the consolidation and sorting, packaging, storage, information flow services make the difference with the competitors in terms of service diversity.
- Using technology to provide services in the right place and at the right time in a fast, high quality and economical way.
- Organizing the services in the port in line with customer needs, as integrated logistics services from a single source quickly, accurately and with high quality. Development of robust information systems to support all operational processes.
- Attracting the attention of the customer with business focus, flexible cost structure, effective inventory management, reduction in warehouse management expenses, high storage and security standards, zero investment requirement, liquid ability of existing investments, use of up-to-date logistics technologies and information systems.
- Reducing total operational costs and improving the process by integrating transportation services with other services and solving problems instantly with fast communication from a single source.
- Realizing the project and operations management and process follow-up from a single source in accordance with the needs of the customers.

Chapter 14

Tube Packaging Co.

The company was founded in 1955 to develop unique packaging solutions that contribute to the commercial success of its customers. The company established its first factory in 1957 to produce slug and aluminum tubes. Renewing its production lines with advanced technologies by incorporating technical competencies such as aluminum Monoblock aerosol can production, aluminum barrier laminated tube production, plastic barrier laminated tube production, the company offers global and local customers in the pharma, personal care, cosmetics, home care, food and chemistry/stationery sectors, serves with its high production capacity.

Trends Affecting the Sector

In the brainstorming sessions, the following results were obtained by reviewing the trends of external factors such as demographic, economic, legal-political, technological and social changes, market dynamics, customer expectations, competitive conditions, strategies and objectives of competitors, suppliers, substitutes to the tube package production sector over the next five years:

- The transition from aluminum tube to laminated tube has already reached to its saturation.
- As the war economy continues, the tube will be needed.

DOI: 10.4324/9781003519614-16

- Can the present and future of the sector change in terms of the use of aluminum tubes? How does change act?
- Although tube consumption information in North America, South America, Europe, China, India, Far East is not clear, it is assumed that the tube market is growing by 6% every year.
- It is seen that the share of the tube in the general packaging sector is small.
- It seems that there is no compromise in the above-mentioned tube associations either.
- It is observed that the share of aluminum tubes in the pharmaceutical sector is increasing.
- In oral care, it is seen that the transition from aluminum tube to laminated tube is over.
- PE tubes will continue to grow in their dynamism.
- In pomades and ointments, if the packaging turns into a tablet what would be its effect on the aluminum tube?
- The feasibility of switching to primary packaging, especially in the case of oral care?
- Advantages and disadvantages of returning to primary packaging in medicine?
- The future of sanctions because of the sensitivity of environmental organizations around the world?
- In non-recyclable products, environmental costs will increase and based on this, it will be necessary to turn into larger packaging.
- In parallel with the environmental concerns, there will be a shift to the aluminum tube production.
- Aerosol cylinders, which are also currently used in beer, will be more involved in the packaging industry with the increase in alcohol consumption.
- In the event of the occurrence of depression, the dispensability of aluminum and laminated tubes?
- Identification of the threats that await the sector in the case of the shortages of aluminum raw materials.
- Although merging happened between the producers of aluminum raw materials, there is still no change in pricing and production is at the same pace.
- Due to the use of aluminum raw material in different sectors, it will be difficult to supply the raw material at the required time.

- Since there is a transition from tin to aerosol tubes, there will be problems in the supply of raw materials.
- Due to the changes that may occur in the geography that we are in, is it possible to switch to laminated tube?
- How real is it that multinational companies can produce their own tube needs?
- It is foreseen that the Indian and Chinese markets will increase the prices of raw materials and therefore change the trading conditions in the near future, due to the increase in the life standards of their societies.
- Firms will return to their original business.
- It is thought that private label products can have an important share in market.
- Will the private label be able to maintain its place in the market in the future?
- Can external procurement be perceived as a threat?
- How does the fact that large companies produce their own packages affect the share in the market?
- Without new investments and machinery supply, it may be possible to gather the customers (working within their plants) under one roof.
- Due to the positive signals in Turkey's economy, foreign investors will be able to cooperate here.
- How accurate and profitable can it be to gather tube manufacturers in Turkey under one roof?
- In terms of tube usage, the market in Turkey is still considered to be untouched.
- It is seen that customers are becoming increasingly conscious and competition conditions may change accordingly.
- In some segments, it is seen that product specifications take precedence over price.
- Product continuity, technological competence and standardization are gaining importance.
- Due to the fluctuations in demand, it is thought that domestic production will not be possible in today's conditions with the shortages of basic raw materials.
- Failure to meet the world-class environmental expectations may create legal problems in the future.

- Basic expectation is supplementing equal prices with the same quality and without lowering quality to everyone and every segment.
- From the customer's point of view, the expectation is mainly the issue of pricing and financing. Can quality be compromised?
- Is there a possibility that the sector will expand into new segments?
- The expectation of each segment will be in a different direction. What should be done about it? (e.g., cheap tube.)
- Is it possible to reduce the cost of supplying goods using high technology? Can solidarity be established between the manufacturer and the supplier and a solution can be reached in this regard?
- It is thought that countries such as Korea, China, etc. may invest in nearby regions and Turkey may be under threat in this regard.
- By listening the customers, it will be easier to be in a positive trend in the sector.
- Roll-on will replace aerosol in the near future for safety reasons.
- Can the adhesive industry put larger volumes, instead of aluminum tubes, in glass or plastic bottles?
- The fact that it is supported from the outside indicates that Turkey's political stability will continue.
- Economic growth must continue so that the sector is not negatively affected.
- In the event of an economic crisis, due to the change in foreign exchange, only exporting companies increase their profitability. Otherwise, they fail.
- What are the consequences of eliminating Turkey from the European customs union?
- Technological developments affect the speed of operations.
- Due to the change in geometry in the aerosol, tool investments are essential.
- Investment is essential to be competitive in the sector.
- Depending on the request of the end user, if a high volume of sales is aimed, it should be acted upon by considering its feasibility.
- Depending on the desire of the end user, not the packaging but the brand comes to the forefront.
- In product selection, criteria can be considered in terms of habit, effect on unit cost, functional convenience and environmental impact.
- The standards demanded by the customer and its existence in the market must be maintained.

Positive/Negative Scenarios

The potential positive and negative scenarios for the tube packaging production sector for the next five years are set out in the following definitions, as a result of group works, taking into account the above-mentioned worldwide and nationwide significant developments in the sector.

Positive Scenarios

- Consumer and environmental awareness (e.g., 100% recycling of aluminum tubes.)
- Innovation ability of the industry.
- It is foreseen that there will be no serious alternative to tube packaging in the near future due to the price advantage and high R&D prices for alternative products.
- Increase on the diversity of use within the sector, and accordingly the need for the formation of new segments.
- The increase in the population and welfare level both in the world and Turkey and their positive impact on demand.
- Positive effects of the commercial growth in B2B on the sector.

Negative Scenarios

- The investment amount is relatively low and the tubes that require little know-how can be produced within the customer.
- In particular, the inability to recycle laminated tubes, additional investments that are considered mandatory, and legal sanctions related to environmental issues will increase.
- The negative reflection of the increase in raw material prices on the sector.
- The fact that the labor force wants an increasing share of the marginal profit.
- The challenges that the development of new types of packaging will pose to existing ones.

Evolution of the Organization

1955   Established.

1956   The company was established by Turkish and French joint capital. Gen. Dir. appointed.

1957   The factory started its operations.
        Production of foundries, slugs and aluminum tubes was started.
        Agreed with aluminum supplier.

1958   Aluminum etui, Sn coated lead and Pb tube production was
        started.
        First customers.

1964   Production of two-part bottles and aerosols was started.

1967   Injection cap production was started.

1974   The first automatic lines (17) were received.
        The company transferred to the Turkish capital.

1975   A new General Administrator was appointed.
        A new automatic line was put into operation.
        Monoblock aerosol production and Inc. structure was started.

1977   Initial exportation efforts: Iran and the United Arab Republic.
        Reductions in the production of etui.

1979   Gen. Dir. has changed.
        A workforce of around 500.

1983   Transition to polyester paint.
        Exporting department took into place.
        Began to undergo modernization.

1984   Starting of a rotary casting unit and new slug production facilities.

1985   Workshop modernization.

1986   Acquisition of line 13.

1987   New Gen. Dir.

1990   Reduction in labor force (about 300 people.)

1993   Laminated tube production was put into operation.

1994   The current form of the workforce (~270.)

1995   Exit from etui production.

1997   Physical modernization of the factory and establishment of IT
        infrastructure.
        Relocation of the headquarters to the factory.

1999   ETMA membership.

2000   Investment in automatic cartooning machines.

2001   Transition to production label automation.
        Establishment of a computer-aided ink preparation laboratory.

2002   Obtaining ISO and TSE certificates.
        Transition to the MRP system.

2003   Initial PBL-laminated tube investment.
        Acquisition of the first hole-selection machine.

2004   Transition to the warehouse barcoding system.

2005   Termination of slug production.

2006   Development of occupational health and safety regulations.

Current Status of the Organization

Considering the stages of the enterprise from past to present, the following results were obtained through brainstorming and group studies in order to determine the strengths and weaknesses they have created in the business structure. In this study, internal factors such as workforce, technology, organization and management, operational issues, products and market positions, financial characteristics, etc. are taken into consideration. In addition, the strengths and weaknesses of the organization were compared with the skills of the main competitors and the success factors of the industry to determine its competitive advantages.

- Integration is achieved in tube production.
- Moved into the international markets.
- Increased specialization.
- Became a high-quality brand.
- Became a leader in its sector.
- There have been serious developments in the direction of institutionalization.
- Costs have been made minimizable.
- Able to follow the technological developments in the sector with its own resources.
- Manpower turnover is minimized.

- Easily reachable top management.
- Its current technology has become efficient.
- According to Etma data, it is able to be in the top 10 in every year.
- The management performance has reached up to good levels.
- Due to the intensity in customer orders, the demand for a long-term program from customers has caused distress to customers, thus causing the usual flexibility, delivery time and also cost not to be in the preferred position.
- A staff has already gained a certain amount of experience (however, they should always be open to improvement).
- Supplier accessibility and relationships have been improved.
- Ability to create finance.
- Able to keep up with the changes that could occur in aluminum tubes.
- Established brand awareness and standards in the domestic market.
- Especially for the large-volume orders from abroad, definitely being considered as an important supplier among the others.
- Able to perceive and adapt to environmental developments.
- In terms of resilience to the economic crisis, a strong financial structure and the ability to react by its own structure have emerged.

Strengths

- Low employee turnover.
- Quality of products and services.
- To be good in the domestic market and known in the international market.
- A solid financial structure.
- Efficient cost and budget tracking system and good management of working capital.
- Operational efficiency.
- Efficient corporate structure.

Weaknesses

- Insufficient physical conditions of the facility for space and capacity increase.
- Inability to implement the results of the strategic planning system.
- Lack of product diversity in laminated and aerosol tubes.
- Low profit rate.

- The CRM system does not exist.
- Inadequacy in R&D and project development.
- Overseas representative offices are not established.
- Dependence on suppliers and risks taken in the main inputs, as well as high costs.
- Supplier relations.
- Inadequate performance-enhancing incentives.
- Lack of multi-facility although it is necessary.

Competitive Advantages

- Experience
- To be in a leading position in the domestic market.
- Wide portfolio distribution.
- Infrastructure suitable for economies of scale.
- Price
- Ability to self-criticize.
- Geographical status

Future Design of the Organization

Opportunities for the organization (taking into account the competitive advantages of the enterprise and matching them with potential positive scenarios of the sector) and therefore the strategic objective, main goals and main strategies to be achieved over the next five years are determined by the brainstorming and group work sessions.

Organization's Opportunity Definition

- Large quantity orders (all segments for aluminum and laminated tubes in the Balkans and the Middle East.)
- International demand (Europe, North Africa, USA – all segments.)
- New investment plans of multinational companies.
- OTC drugs
- Retaining loyal customers by improving cooperation.
- Obtaining markets identified as opportunities (Balkans, Middle East) through investment or cooperation.
- Developing markets by providing low price, high product quality, high service quality within short deadlines.

Strategic Objective

To be the solution partner preferred by all companies that use and can use tube packaging by offering the most appropriate responses to their needs.

Main Goals

Market Goals (geographical, sectoral):

- Develop cooperation with suppliers.
- Europe (stationery, pharmaceuticals, food, cosmetics – with aluminum and laminated tube).
- North Africa (cosmetics, pharmaceuticals – with aluminum and laminated tube).
- Middle East (pharmaceutical, cosmetic, stationery – with aluminum tube).
- CBT (cosmetic, pharmaceutical – with aluminum and laminated tube).
- America (stationery, OTC, pharmaceutical – mainly laminated).

Investment Goals:

- Establishment of a new plant in Bulgaria (possibly Eastern Europe).
- Move the existing plant capacity to a place deemed appropriate.
- Produce laminated tubes at the customer site who needs high-capacity packaging.
- Commissioning of the plant required for additional capacity in an appropriate way (e.g., acquiring a competitor, physical investment, leasing, cooperation).
- Modernization of existing capacity.
- Creating an alternative slug plant.
- Make the necessary arrangements for the environmental issues.

Collaborations:

- Develop cooperation with suppliers.
- Being able to offer full package with PE tube manufacturers.
- Provide joint solutions in cooperation with customers.

Financial Goals:

- Develop a systematic approach to cost reduction.

Organizational Goals:

- Establishment of a customer evaluation system.
- Development of existing segments.
- Creating the image that it should be.
- Form the sales organization from regional sales representatives and/or representative offices in the necessary regions.

Main Strategies

In the light of the opportunities and main goals identified above, and according to the "components of strategy" (Ansoff 1970), it seems appropriate that the preference of the enterprise in the product-market position should be to develop new nearby markets with existing products. Therefore, *market development* is one of the main strategies.

Market development:

- After the research, create an external structure that will follow proactive sales activities. This strategy may include office and/or team building with a focus on Europe and the UK.
- Increase company awareness.
- Carry out promotional activities professionally (participation in fairs, designing efficient web site, etc.).

Referring to the "general competitive strategies" (Porter 1998), the most basic competitive advantage of this enterprise is its low cost and a narrower scope rather than global as a field of activity that seems appropriate. So, *cost focusing* is another of its main strategies.

Cost focusing:

- Operational excellence.
- Reducing waste with improvements to be made and reducing unit costs with efficiency-increasing solutions.
- Economies of scale (with capacity increase and technology upgrade).
- Install the TPM system and make it operational.
- Keeping personnel costs under control.
- Improving inventory turnover rates and aging.
- Synergy in purchasing.

- Reviewing all processes all over and designing more productive systems by taking process management training and consultancy services.
- Establish a backup and development system for key positions.
- Recruit employees with sufficient competencies for additional blue-collar personnel needs and subject them to continuous training and certification together with existing employees.
- Establish a system for high-performance employees receiving premiums.
- Planning lean layout and material handling systems for the existing factory and warehouse facilities.
- Using green factory energy-saving concepts in new investment.

Chapter 15

Vocational Training Organization

It is a vocational education institution that is in the initial stage with the aim of making young people in Turkey have professional competencies at international standards.

Trends Affecting the Sector

The effects of external factors such as demographic, economic, legal-political, technological and social changes, market dynamics, customer expectations, competitive conditions, strategies and targets of competitors, suppliers and substitutes on the vocational training over the next five years were reviewed in brainstorming sessions and the following results were obtained:

- Education on the internet and on a university basis can be developed in the most appropriate way.
- Education should be face-to-face in the true sense and the internet should be used as a tool.
- Unemployment of university graduates is increasing.
- $380 per person spent on all-inclusive education in Turkey, $3,500 in OECD, $2,800 in Greece and $785 in Zimbabwe.
- A total of 65% of those who win university education win through tutoring.

DOI: 10.4324/9781003519614-17

- High schools in Turkey cannot prepare students for university.
- A total of 70% of those who have won the university are those who have waited for a year, 20% are recent graduates, and 10% are those who are studying at the university.
- Effective methods must be found for students' learning.
- The targeted students may be those who have graduated from high school and waited a year or more to get into university.
- The number of young people who have studied abroad in Turkey is increasing day by day, and this situation is no longer a plus feature. The sought-after trait was communication skills and positive behavior.
- A large proportion of high school graduates are from public schools and only 2% graduated from private schools.
- Laws oppose the development of private schools (high taxes, etc.)
- Purchasing power is low and accordingly it affects education negatively.
- The state may try to improve the quality of existing schools through education policy.
- Private schools tend to provide vocational skills.
- A student who goes to a straight high school can take courses from any vocational school within the provincial borders.
- National Education Law in Turkey is modern, but its applicability is weak.
- The average duration of education in Turkey is 5.7 years.
- The market for private schools is open at the saleable price.
- Educators need to be trained.
- Career inventories need to be created in order to define sectoral competencies and to train human resources suitable for these competencies.
- Based on the developments in the world, the need for workforce should be determined.
- The automotive industry is shifting from developed countries to developing countries.
- The need for manpower in the textile sector will increase, but the rate of illegal workforce in the sector is very high.
- The need for qualified manpower in the tourism sector in Turkey is very high.
- The leather and footwear industry in Turkey has a clear path ahead.
- There is great potential in light and heavy manufacturing.

- The construction industry needs different types of workforces.
- The state's policy regarding educational institutions is weak.
- Although there are qualified teaching staff in Anatolia, this staff cannot be valued professionally. On the other hand, it is very difficult to find teaching staff in Istanbul due to the difficult living conditions.
- Businessmen in Turkey are trying to make investments abroad in relation to education.
- Countries in Europe where Turks live intensely have a high market capacity.
- There is a need for an organized work in the promotion and marketing of Turkey's business lines.
- There is a development in the world to receive services from qualified and cheap workforce like Turkey, for example, call centers.
- There is a great potential for people who want to receive short-term vocational training in Turkey, especially from Germany. Its justification is cheapness, proximity to culture, etc.
- Vocational courses of universities are very intense.

Positive/Negative Scenarios

The potential positive and negative scenarios for the vocational training sector over the next five years are set out in the following definitions, as a result of group works, taking into account the above-mentioned worldwide and nationwide significant developments in the sector.

Positive Scenarios

- The public and private sectors are ready and vocational training activities are on their agenda.
- A large number of people are looking for the future and a place to trust.
- Companies are looking for sectoral-based skilled employees.
- The EU accession is progressing positively and there are concrete supports, such as the 6th framework program.
- Domestic and foreign training activities that are at a saleable price, which include employment guarantees, are attracted.
- There is a sufficient level of education forces available. At the local level, career centers are open.

Negative Scenarios

- The financial power of the people who want to receive education is weak and they need support.
- There are a few tried models and success stories.
- A large number of players want to take part in the market.
- The existence of foreign education programs that are not suitable for the conditions of Turkey has a negative impact on the market.
- There are stories of failures due to training programs that have no guarantee of employment, and this decreases demand.
- If you are not corporate, professional, reliable and foreign-sourced, negativities may occur.

Current Status of the Organization

Considering the current status of the enterprise which is in the introductory stage, the following results were obtained through brainstorming and group studies in order to determine the strengths that they have created in the business structure.

Strengths

- The team consists of individual strengths with experience, creativity, know-how, university and private-public sector connections, and domestic-international relations.
- Capabilities to create synergy.
- Possibility to combine financial power with creativity to create a geometric increase.
- Sharing common values.
- Ease of access to the staff.
- Connections to offer employment opportunities abroad.

Future Design of the Organization

In the light of the results obtained in the above studies, the opportunities and accordingly the main goals and strategies to be achieved for the organization for the next five years are indicated by the brainstorming and group work.

Organization's Opportunity Definition

The demand for higher education in Turkey is increasing. If this demand for education cannot be met, young people turn to the business world to find a job. From this point of view, students who cannot enter higher education will have the opportunity if professions can be provided to them by being in cooperation with the business world.

Main Goals

Targeted Market and Market Goals:

- Students who cannot enter higher education or who have graduated from high school and vocational high schools by passing vocational schools without an exam.
- Istanbul and regions close to Istanbul.
- Developed regions.
- Selected sectors and leading organizations.

Operational and Technological Goals:

- Distance education.
- Hands-on and on-site training with the leading companies of the sector and thus prepare them for business life.
- Establishing career, personal development and learning centers.
- Building strong relationships with employment agencies and financial institutions.

Main Strategies

In the light of the opportunities and main goals set out above, and according to the "components of strategy" (Ansoff 1970), it seems appropriate that the preference of this entrepreneurial enterprise, which is at the introductory stage, in the product-market position is to develop the existing market by providing necessary training programs. Therefore, *market penetration* (in cooperation with national/international educational organizations) is one of the main strategies.

According to "general competitive strategies" (Porter 1998), by knowing that innovation and differentiation as the main competitive advantages of this enterprise and focusing initially on a narrower scope as an area of marketing activity, *differentiation focusing* seems to be another appropriate strategy for this firm.

Chapter 16

Building Materials Producer

Company, which was founded for the production of industrial lime, has been upgraded into offering a complementary business and product model that makes the consumer's life easier in building materials.

Company has undertaken the leadership of machine applied plaster sector in the Turkish market with its innovative and pioneering approach. The company's product range consists of gypsum-based plasters (ABS), cement-based plasters (CBS), decorative plasters, technical mortars, waterproofing products, thermal insulation products, tile adhesives and joint fillers, lime and aggregate product groups.

Environmental Analysis

The effects of external factors such as demographic, economic, legal-political, technological and social changes, market dynamics, customer expectations, competitive conditions, strategies and objectives of competitors, etc. on the machine applied plaster sector were reviewed in brainstorming and group study sessions and by using statistical techniques of forecasting.

Macroeconomic Analysis

Macroeconomic variables affect enterprises and the industries in which they are functioning and are not under the control of the enterprises.

DOI: 10.4324/9781003519614-18

Macroeconomic variables are as follows:

- Demographical
- Economical
- Legal-Political
- Technological
- Social-Cultural

This analysis was carried out in relation to the region and the country to find out the effects of macroeconomic variables on the sector. The effects of macroeconomic variables on the machine applied plaster sector were reviewed by statistical techniques of forecasting.

Statistical Model for Quantitative Impact of Macro-Economical Variables (Regression Model)

As far as the dynamics of construction industry and construction materials sub-sector are concerned, the primary factors affecting supply and demand growth in the sector are:

- GNP growth rate.
- Growth in number of households.
- Population growth rate.
- Growth in number of licensed buildings.
- Increase in unit of buildings.

The following involves the projection of these five factors, taking as a basis the past 20 years (see Table 16.1). Forecasts were obtained to be taken as the denominator of each factor. These reveal the forecasts of trends for future rates as well as the number of licensed apartments that form the numerator in each rate. Often an arithmetic mean of these rates may be used.

$$y = -411.7 + 0.1117x_1 + 1.526\ x_2 + 0.1236x_3 + 1.8409\ x_4 + 0.3820x_5$$

$R^2 = 0{,}968$

X_1: Growth of GNP per capita
X_2: Growth in number of households
X_3: Population growth
X_4: Growth in number of licensed buildings
X_5: Increase in unit m^2 building prices

Table 16.1   Forecast of Macroeconomic Changes

Years	Licensed No. of Flats Growth (000) (y)	GNP per Capita Increase (000) (xl)	Growth House Holds (x2)	Pop. Growth Rate (x3)	Licensed Build. Growth (x4)	Building m2 Price Increase (x5)
1977	216	11	295	853	25	6
1978	237	−11	307	872	26	44
1979	252	−31	323	890	31	33
1980	204	−57	330	908	32	−49
1981	144	26	229	1102	27	−19
1982	160	6	235	1148	49	−7
1983	169	20	242	1176	37	−3
1984	189	53	247	1206	38	−6
1985	259	22	255	1236	77	13
1986	393	56	276	1127	143	17
1987	498	99	283	1128	160	−1
1988	474	−10	292	1154	168	7
1989	413	−8	300	1178	132	19
1990	381	96	308	1205	71	30
1991	393	−24	317	1228	77	21
1992	473	66	326	1258	123	7
1993	548	95	335	1285	136	5
1994	524	−128	345	1314	132	−46
1995	508	92	355	1343	99	15
1996	446	91	364	1372	94	−1

Analysis of Industry Forces

The forces that most influence a business are the groups that makeup competition within the industry in which it operates:

- Competition between companies involved in the industry.
- The threat of potential new firms.
- Customers' bargaining power.
- The threat of substitute products.
- The power of suppliers.
- Other interest profits (government, trade associations, financiers, etc.).

The effectiveness of these forces determines the intensity of competition in an industry. This analysis was carried out by different working groups and shows the summary status of the effects of the competitive forces on the machine applied plaster sector for the next five years.

Rivalry

COMPETITION of EXISTING BUSINESSES	ABS	CBS	
Number of existing firms	<15	<10	
Industry growth rate	10%	10%	
Product characteristics difference	NO	NO	
Service	YES	YES	
Fixed costs	5	3	Costs evaluated on a scale of 5
Industry exit cost	<6M$	<1M$	

- For ABS, the level of competition is high despite the low number of businesses operating in the sector due to other factors.
- For CBS, although competition among businesses is expected to be low, it is high because of the price pressure created by traditional plaster.

New Players

THREAT of NEW BUSINESSES	ABS	CBS	
Number of big firms	11	4	
Brand recognition	NO	NO	
Entry cost	<6M$	<2M$	
Difficulty of reaching distribution channels	4	4	Degree of difficulty evaluated on a scale of 5
Cost advantages	5	4	Degree of advantage evaluated on a scale of 5
Government barriers	4	1	Degree of difficulty evaluated on a scale of 5

- For ABS, the possibility of new players to threaten existing businesses in the sector is low.

■ For CBS, although the possibility of new players to threaten existing businesses in the sector seems to be high, new entrants would expand the market since industrial plaster has a lower market share relative to traditional plaster.

Customers

POWER of CUSTOMERS	ABS	CBS	
Demand power of customer	5	5	Demand evaluated on a scale of 5
Backward integration potential	1	3	Production potential evaluated on a scale of 5
Alternative sellers	YES	YES	
Brand switching cost	1	1	
Sensitivity on price and service change	5	5	
Satisfaction w.r.t existing products	5	5	

■ Customers are strong for all product groups.

Suppliers

POWER of SUPPLIERS	ABS	CBS
Number of firms in industry	<15	<10
Number of suppliers:		
gypsum and cement	<15	<20
chemical a	5	5
chemical b	<10	<10
packaging	1	6
Forward integration capability	1	1

■ For ABS, gypsum suppliers are not strong.
■ For CBS, cement suppliers are strong.
■ Chemical suppliers are strong in this product group, since they are all global manufacturers.

- Packaging products are monopolistic for ABS.
- None of these suppliers has a structure suitable for advanced integration.

Substitutes

THREAT of SUBSTITUTE PRODUCTS	ABS	CBS
	Plaster board, cement-based plaster	All exterior facade cladding, gypsum, black cement plaster

Machine Applied Plaster Industry Life Cycle (see Figure 16.1.)

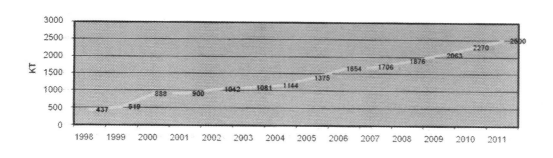

Figure 16.1   Life cycle of machine applied plaster industry.

Positive/Negative Scenarios

The potential positive and negative scenarios for the machine applied plaster sector over the next five years are set out in the following definitions, as a result of group work, taking into account the above-mentioned significant analysis and developments in the sector.

Positive Scenario Definitions

- The expectation that the existing economic stability will be maintained and the arrangements for reducing bureaucracy and taxes lead to an expectation of sustainable 5% growth during the next five years. This climate will result in increased foreign direct investments and will be supported.

■ As a result of the flow of global liquidity from developed country markets to developing country markets, stable and low-cost interest and exchange rates (particularly in nation), the currently rising young population and the support of all these factors with the mortgage law prepared by the government, the demand for housing will grow and the construction industry will assume a growth trend above the economic growth.

■ As a result of standardization in the industry through laws to be enacted by nations in the EU accession process, traditional methods will be replaced by industrial methods. Thus, the market volume of standardized industrial products will increase and the need for know-how in production will bring about sectorial consolidation.

■ It will not be possible to replace advanced technology products, which will emerge as a result of construction technologies following a rapid development trend, with traditional products. Traditional structures will be replaced by rapid and economic solutions to be enabled by new application systems and new strategies enabling direct access to end users.

■ The advantages offered by the geographical position of the nation and her active role in regional countries will allow the industry to expand in the region. Domestic contracting companies that have gained a regional company structure will move national construction material manufacturers into a position of regional manufacturers.

Negative Scenario Definitions

■ Potential negative developments in foreign relations (EU accession process, Cyprus issue, Iraq) will lead to fluctuations and instability in the national economy. Such fluctuation in the economy will lead to weakened purchasing power. This contraction in the market would negatively affect the construction industry.

■ Weakened purchasing power would increase demand for traditional methods and reduce the market of industrial products.

■ The ongoing economic program would be interrupted. Country's borrowing costs would increase and expenditures would diminish.

Devaluation would be inevitable to overcome this contraction in the economy. Devaluation would lead to crisis in sectors using external loans. Furthermore, energy and raw material costs would rise, capacity utilization would decline and prices would surge.

Current Status of the Organization

Considering the stages of the enterprise from past to present, the following results were obtained through brainstorming and group studies in order to determine the strengths and weaknesses they have created in the business structure. In addition, the strengths of the organization are compared with the skills of the main competitors to determine their competitive advantages and success factors.

Strengths and Weaknesses

Table 16.2 shows the internal analysis with a functional approach. In this study, internal factors such as workforce, technology, organization and management, operational issues, products and market positions, financial characteristics, etc. are taken into consideration.

Competitive Advantages and Success Factors

Table 16.3 is a comparison table with the strengths of main competitors that results in the firm's competitive advantages and success factors (Table 16.4). In short, we can say the following:

- Competitive advantages – factors that give the business an advantage over its competitors and key factors on which the strategy of the business will be formed.
- Success factors – important factors that the business must have but are also typically found in every profitable competitor. It does not constitute a potential source for any strategic advantage.
- Key vulnerabilities – factors in which the business does not currently have the necessary skills, knowledge or resources to compete effectively.

Table 16.2 Internal Analysis by Functional Approach

		Factors	*Strengths*	*Weaknesses*
Organization of General Management		1. Flexible and horizontal relations facilitate decision making	☑	
		2. Participatory and sharing management	☑	
		3. Broad investment vision	☑	
		4. Prestigious company name	☑	
		5. Experienced management staff undertaking responsibilities	☑	
		6. Strategic planning and budget discipline	☑	
		7. Organizational climate, culture		☑
		8. There is no continuity in the organization		☑
		9. Sudden decision-making, quick change of decision		☑
Personnel		1. Competent, experienced and responsible staff	☑	
		2. Qualified and young labor force	☑	
		3. Specialized staff	☑	
		4. Effective use of incentives to motivate performance		☑
		5. Employee turnover and absenteeism		☑
		6. No career plan		☑
		7. Stressful environment, fatigue factor		☑
Production & Technical		1. Ease of raw material supply	☑	
		2. Good supplier relations	☑	
		3. Registered trademarks	☑	
		4. Effective use of subcontractors	☑	
		5. Cost advantage through extraction of sand from own sandpit	☑	
		6. Production control procedures	☑	
		7. Effective quality control	☑	
		8. Vertical integration	☑	
		9. Technical team competence	☑	
		10. Layout and utilization of facilities		☑
		11. Research and development		☑
		12. Single-point production and distribution channel		☑
		13. Low-capacity utilization		☑

(Continued)

Table 16.2   Internal Analysis by Functional Approach (*Continued*)

	Factors	Strengths	Weaknesses
Marketing	1. Product diversity	☑	
	2. Market leadership	☑	
	3. Pre-sales application service	☑	
	4. For ABS and CBS - channels of distribution: number, coverage and control	☑	
	5. For ABS and CBS – high quality and branded products	☑	
	6. Technical support department	☑	
	7. Strong references	☑	
	8. After-sale service and follow up	☑	
	9. Concentration of sales in a few products or to a few customers		☑
	10. Ability to gather needed information about markets		☑
	11. For technical products - channels of distribution: number, coverage and control		☑
	12. Effective sales organization		☑
	13. For technical products - product/service image and reputation		☑
	14. Imaginative, efficient and effective sales promotion and advertising		☑
	15. Customer relationship management		☑
Finance & Accounting	1. Automation and integration through system investments, resulting in effective accounting, costing and budgeting	☑	
	2. Effective cost control	☑	
	3. High credibility	☑	
	4. Positive communication with shareholders, strong shareholder structure	☑	
	5. High equity profitability	☑	
	6. High working capital ratio	☑	
	7. High profit margin	☑	
	8. Long-term capital raising capacity	☑	
	9. Image of a tax-paying and strong company	☑	
	10. Financing of investments entirely with equity		☑
	11. High accounts receivable		☑
	12. Failure to secure sales		☑
	13. Inventory management		☑

Table 16.3   Comparison of Strengths with Main Competitors'

	Factors	Co. X	Main Competitors
Organization of General Management	1. Flexible and horizontal relations facilitate decision making	☑	
	2. Participatory and sharing management	☑	
	3. Broad investment vision	☑	☑
	4. Prestigious company name	☑	☑
	5. Experienced management staff undertaking responsibilities	☑	☑
	6. Strategic planning and budget discipline	☑	☑
Personnel	1. Competent, experienced and responsible staff	☑	
	2. Qualified and young labor force	☑	
	3. Specialized staff	☑	☑
Production & Technical	1. Ease of raw material supply	☑	
	2. Good supplier relations	☑	☑
	3. Registered trademarks	☑	
	4. Effective use of subcontractors	☑	
	5. Cost advantage through extraction of sand from own sandpit	☑	
	6. Production control procedures	☑	
	7. Effective quality control	☑	☑
	8. Vertical integration	☑	
	9. Technical team competence	☑	☑
Marketing	1. Product diversity	☑	
	2. Market leadership	☑	
	3. Pre-sales application service	☑	☑
	4. For ABS and CBS - channels of distribution: number, coverage and control	☑	☑
	5. For ABS and CBS – high quality and branded products	☑	
	6. Technical support department	☑	☑
	7. Strong references	☑	☑
	8. After-sale service and follow up	☑	

(Continued)

Table 16.3   Comparison of Strengths with Main Competitors' (*Continued*)

	Factors	Co. X	Main Competitors
Finance & Accounting	1. Automation and integration through system investments, resulting in effective accounting, costing and budgeting	☑	
	2. Effective cost control	☑	☑
	3. High credibility	☑	☑
	4. Positive communication with shareholders, strong shareholder structure	☑	
	5. High equity profitability	☑	
	6. High working capital ratio	☑	
	7. High profit margin	☑	
	8. Long-term capital raising capacity	☑	☑
	9. Image of a tax-paying and strong company	☑	

Table 16.4   Competitive Advantages and Success Factors

	Factors	Competitive Advantages	Success Factors
Organization of General Management	1. Flexible and horizontal relations facilitate decision making	☑	
	2. Participatory and sharing management	☑	
	3. Broad investment vision		☑
	4. Prestigious company name		☑
	5. Experienced management staff undertaking responsibilities		☑
	6. Strategic planning and budget discipline		☑
Personnel	1. Competent, experienced and responsible staff	☑	
	2. Qualified and young labor force	☑	
	3. Specialized staff		☑

(*Continued*)

Table 16.4   Competitive Advantages and Success Factors (*Continued*)

	Factors	Competitive Advantages	Success Factors
Production & Technical	1. Ease of raw material supply	☑	
	2. Good supplier relations		☑
	3. Registered trademarks	☑	
	4. Effective use of subcontractors	☑	
	5. Cost advantage through extraction of sand from own sandpit	☑	
	6. Production control procedures	☑	
	7. Effective quality control		☑
	8. Vertical integration	☑	
	9. Technical team competence		☑
Marketing	1. Product diversity	☑	
	2. Market leadership	☑	
	3. Pre-sales application service		☑
	4. For ABS and CBS - channels of distribution: number, coverage and control		☑
	5. For ABS and CBS – high quality and branded products	☑	
	6. Technical support department		☑
	7. Strong references		☑
	8. After-sale service and follow up	☑	
Finance & Accounting	1. Automation and integration through system investments, resulting in effective accounting, costing and budgeting	☑	
	2. Effective cost control		☑
	3. High credibility		☑
	4. Positive communication with shareholders, strong shareholder structure	☑	
	5. High equity profitability	☑	
	6. High working capital ratio	☑	
	7. High profit margin	☑	
	8. Long-term capital raising capacity		☑
	9. Image of a tax-paying and strong company	☑	

Future Design of the Organization

Opportunities for the organization (taking into account the competitive advantages of the enterprise and matching them with potential positive scenarios of the sector – Table 16.5), and therefore the main goals and main strategies to be achieved over the next five years are indicated by the brainstorming and group work sessions.

Organization's Opportunity Definition

Increase in foreign investments would boost competitiveness and expand market volume. Furthermore, scenarios reveal that the positive conclusion of the EU accession process would reduce black cement-based plaster penetration. In the gypsum-based plaster sector, market volume is expected to reach 8,400 Kton by 2014. The anticipated sales quantity in the market is 2,500 Kton, which accounts for 24% of market volume. Our firm will capture a market share of 12% thanks to its advanced R&D, prestigious trademark, experienced staff and rapid investment capability.

   Increase in foreign investments would boost competitiveness and expand market volume. Furthermore, scenarios reveal that the positive conclusion of the EU accession process would reduce black cement-based plaster penetration. In the cement-based plaster sector, market volume is expected to reach 36,200 Kton by 2014. The anticipated sales of industrial plasters is 525 Kton. Our firm will capture a market share of 47% in 2011 thanks to its prestigious trademark and experienced staff.

Main Goals

Financial and Market Goals:

- Turnover will be 200 million $, and profitability will be 38 million $in 2014.
- Entering new markets: Balkans, Russia, Cyprus, Ukraine and North Africa.
- Increasing brand recognition.
- Customer relations management and customer-oriented sales.
- Developing new products (plaster board, technical mortars and liquids).

Table 16.5   Opportunities – Matching Competitive Advantages with Positive Scenarios

	Positive Scenarios	Competitive Advantages	Definition of Opportunities	Reactions of Competitors
Scenario A	**A. Foreign investment will increase**	GM1, F4, F7	With the increase in foreign investments, there will be an increase in industrial materials.	Opponents will take their own positions.
	A1. Reduction of bureaucracy			
	A2. Reduction of taxes			
	A3. Positive economic prospects			
	A4. Political stability			
Scenario B	**B. Increase in construction sector**	GM1, M1, M2, M5, M6	As the sector grows, the demand for differentiated products will increase. Housing demand will boost sales.	The fact that competitors are foreign partners limits their mobility. It will take measures to increase sales.
	B2. Young population, housing needs, zoning laws, low exchange rate			
	B3. Mortgage			
Scenario C	**C. EU relations**	GM1, M1, M2, F4, F7	Demand for industrial products will increase. Merging with suitable companies will expand the market.	Competitors may switch to the use of subcontractors.
	C1. Illegal production will fall, traditional products will fall			
	C2. Sectoral consolidation			

(*Continued*)

Table 16.5 Opportunities – Matching Competitive Advantages with Positive Scenarios (*Continued*)

	Positive Scenarios	Competitive Advantages	Definition of Opportunities	Reactions of Competitors
Scenario D	**D. Developments in construction technologies and communication**	GM1, P1, F4, F7, M2, M5, M6	The market will be enlarged by ensuring the standard in production quality.	They will want to have sources of raw materials. They will take the advantage of being international.
	D1. Quality construction materials, renovation products			
	D2. Development of new products and systems			
	D3. Industrial plaster will increase			
Scenario E	**E. Opening up to foreign markets**	P1, F4, F7, S2, S5, S6	Opening up to foreign markets will grow the sector and will increase our share.	Most of them exist in target markets.

Operational and Organizational Goals:

- Making new investments: Defined domestic and overseas locations.
- Raising productivity to 85% and shortening/speeding up the production process through technology investments.
- Optimizing and improving costs.
- Maintaining/improving product quality and attaining 5 Sigma.
- Raising capacity utilization rate to 70%.

Main Strategies

In the light of the opportunities and main goals identified above, and according to the "components of strategy" (Ansoff 1970), the preference of the enterprise in the product-market position for the domestic and overseas markets are mentioned as shown in the following paragraphs.

Domestic:

	Concentration	Market Development	Product Development	Honzontal Integration
ABS	A+B+C	A	A+B	A
CBS	A+C	B	B	

Concentration

A – doing business in existing markets with existing products.

B – ensuring that existing customers are utilized at a greater scale.

C – making the customers without any consumption habit yet ready for consumption.

Market development

A – offering existing products to new markets.

B – entering new segments as market.

Product development

A – adding new features to existing products.

B – improving the quality structure of existing products.

Horizontal integration

A – acquisition of competitors.

Overseas:

■ Investing/purchasing in regions with security and strategic importance.

■ Establishing joint-ventures with strong companies in their region or opening branches/leasing.

Chapter 17

Application Service Provider (ASP)

To meet the technology and know-how needs of existing and/or potential ASPs, the organization aims to leverage its trusted brand, know-how, nationwide infrastructure, and strategic partnerships by achieving market leadership in providing all the necessary services that come with being a one-stop-shopping ASP enabler. In doing so, the company always aims to maintain its position as a reliable, successful, fast, brand-agnostic, and inexpensive ASP enabler.

Trends Affecting the Sector

The effects of external factors such as demographic, economic, legal-political, technological and social changes, market dynamics, customer expectations, competitive conditions, strategies and targets of competitors, suppliers and substitutes on the application service provision sector over the next five years were reviewed in brainstorming sessions and the following results were obtained:

- The ASP market in the world will be rapidly growing.
- A software-heavy approach will be developed.
- The number of players in the ASP market will decrease.
- It is becoming important for ASP companies to provide value-added services.

DOI: 10.4324/9781003519614-19

- The ASP market will thrive as complementary players form strategic partnerships.
- In the ASP market, there are players that provide simple solutions for the end users, as well as players that add value for the organizations. Players who provide services for institutions choose to gather their solutions under their brands in order to ensure the trust expectation of the users.
- The presentation of mission-critical applications in ASP logic has gradually started to be accepted by users.
- Software companies want to be ASP.
- There is a need for players who can add value to ASP.
- Instead of offering a general solution, it will become necessary to gather the best solutions on different issues in order to take part in the market.
- Consulting companies either want to become ASPs themselves or benefit from ASP by being under the umbrella of other ASPs. Because of their industry-specific knowledge, they can provide business consultancy.
- Industry-specific solutions will be adopted.
- Information technologies have become a serious factor in competitiveness. Its use has become widespread. Small companies have also become needy.
- Time has become of the essence. Therefore, a ready-made solution has become more preferable than an ideal solution.
- It has become important to outsource information and know-how.
- The communication infrastructure has come to support the central organization. Information technology has become complex. In other words, the centralized solution is preferred.
- In Turkey, E-business and ASP concepts can be presented together.
- Although there is a great need for an ASP solution in Turkey, the demand has not yet arisen at a sufficient rate due to the lack of recognition of the concept.
- There is a tendency to imitate what someone else is doing.
- Big companies will make up the economy. Therefore, it is necessary to position yourself to the market with a solution offered to a big company and make a name out of it.
- The number of SMEs in Turkey will decrease.
- SMEs' interest in IT will increase over time.
- Organizations don't rely on others to deliver their applications.
- Turkey's telecom infrastructure is a disadvantage for the ASP model.

- Privatization will not bring change in Turkey.
- The shift to ASP will happen earlier in small organizations that haven't switched to IT.
- Uncertainty about suppliers in Turkey will continue. These uncertainties can be turned in a positive direction.
- It will be important for success to provide training for the services to be offered.
- The financial advantages provided by the ASP model are more advantageous in Turkey.

Positive/Negative Scenarios

The potential positive and negative scenarios for the application service provision sector over the next five years are set out in the following definitions, as a result of group works, taking into account the above-mentioned worldwide and nationwide significant developments in the sector.

Positive Scenarios

- In the ASP market, there are players that provide simple solutions for the end users, as well as players that add value for the organizations. Players who provide services for institutions choose to gather their solutions under their brands in order to ensure the trust expectation of the users.
- Information technologies have become seriously affected by competitiveness and cost. Its use has become widespread. Small companies have also become needy.
- It has become important to outsource information and know-how.
- Big customers see the opportunities this model will provide and support the ASP model.

Negative Scenarios

- Demand from SMEs may be low (they don't rely on others to deliver their applications).
- Turkey's telecom infrastructure will not provide a very wide access network.

- Software companies want to be ASP. Consultancy companies either want to become ASPs themselves or they get the opportunity to be ASP by being under the umbrella of other ASPs. Because of their industry-specific knowledge, they can provide business consultancy.
- Stories of failure.

Current Status of the Organization

Considering the stages of the enterprise from past to present, the following results were obtained through brainstorming and group studies in order to determine the strengths and weaknesses that they have created in the business structure. In this study, internal factors such as workforce, technology, organization and management, operational issues, products and market positions, financial characteristics, etc. are taken into consideration.

Strengths

- Its know-how and infrastructure.
- Established strategic partnerships.
- Projected-sales strategy.
- The company name inspires confidence.
- Having capital power.

Weaknesses

1. Lack of human resources.
2. The organization is not settled as desired.
3. Lack of potential customers.
4. Its services are expensive compared to the market.

Future Design of the Organization

In the light of the results obtained in the above studies, the main goals and main strategies to be achieved for the organization for the next five years are indicated by the brainstorming and group work.

Main Goals

Three separate alternative main goals have been identified:

Alternative 1: Providing only hosting services. The company will be the backbone provider. The most important advantage of this approach is that it does not involve risk, as the sale is made by software companies.

Alternative 2: Selling by developing a sector-specific solution. If the approach is adopted, the risk to the company increases. Also, the biggest disadvantage is that it is a brand-dependent approach.

Alternative 3: The firm will be the ASP enabler. The company's goal is to serve ASPs.

Targeted Market:

- In the case of Alternative1 adoption, software firms such as Logo and SAP.
- In the case of Alternative 2 adopted, large companies that have a chain (companies that are already brick and mortar such as P&G, Unilever, or companies that will act as an interface between us and the chain).
- In the case of Alternative 3 adoption, customers who want to become ASP or customers who would benefit from having ASP.

Market and Financial Goals:

- To achieve the largest market share.
- To support the creation of an information society, the rapid and economical use of new technologies and the optimal use of resources.
- To increase the volume of operations and reduce costs and thus to make new investments.
- Economies of scale (benefits of being able to serve multiple ASPs at the same time.)
- To be able to establish a network of relations throughout Turkey.
- To provide customers with the one-stop-shopping advantage of offering services from a single source (providing complementary services).
- To be reliable, fast and cheap.

Main Strategies

In the light of the main goals set out above, and according to the "components of strategy" (Ansoff 1970), it seems appropriate that the preference of this entrepreneurial enterprise, which is at the introductory stage, in the product-market position is to develop new nearby markets with innovative services. Therefore, *diversification* is one of the main strategies.

According to "general competitive strategies" (Porter 1998), by knowing that innovation and differentiation as the main competitive advantages of this enterprise and focusing initially on a narrower scope as an area of marketing activity, *differentiation focusing* seems to be another appropriate strategy for this firm.

References

Ansoff, H. I. 1970. *Corporate strategy.* London: Penguin.

Bütüner, H. 2015. *Systematic strategic planning: A comprehensive framework for implementation, control and evaluation.* New York: CRC Press.

Harrison, J. S. and C. H. St. John, 2001. *Foundations in strategic management.* Evansville: South-Western Publications.

Muther, R. 2011. *Planning by design.* Kansas City: Institute for High Performance Planners.

Pearce, J. and R. Robinson. 2011. *Strategic management: Formulation, implementation and control.* Columbus: McGraw-Hill Higher Education.

Porter, M. E. 1998. *Competitive strategy: Techniques for analyzing industries and competitors.* Florence: The Free Press.

Vernon, R. 1979. The product cycle hypothesis in a new international environment. *Oxford Bulletin of Economics and Statistics* 41 (4): 255–267.

Wickham, P. A. 2004. *Strategic entrepreneurship.* London: Pearson Education Limited.

Index

Note: Page numbers in *italics* and **bold** refer to figures and tables, respectively.

Printed in the United States
by Baker & Taylor Publisher Services